Testimony of a Resistance Fighter

Raymond Heymann

Published by Raymond Heymann, 2024.

While every precaution has been taken in the preparation of this book, the publisher assumes no responsibility for errors or omissions, or for damages resulting from the use of the information contained herein.

TESTIMONY OF A RESISTANCE FIGHTER

First edition. January 23, 2024.

Copyright © 2024 Raymond Heymann.

ISBN: 979-8224876129

Written by Raymond Heymann.

Testimony of a Resistance Fighter

My Story as a Resistance Fighter in France During World War II

RAYMOND HEYMANN

ChapTER 1

An Alsatian Family Between the World Wars

My name is Raymond Heymann. I was born in Strasbourg in 1919, a city marked by history, just after the conclusion of the Treaty of Versailles.

Strasbourg, this city where the echo of each stone tells a story, where every alley seems to whisper tales of the past. My roots are deeply anchored in Alsace, the land of my ancestors for generations. My parents, my grandparents, my great-grandparents, all were born on this land, woven into the rich tapestry of Alsatian history.

The Judaism of Alsace, to which my family belongs, is a branch of the Jewish tradition that extends along the Rhine Valley. From Basel to the Dutch border, it is characterized by dispersion in small localities. Jewish history in Alsace is complex, marked by prohibitions and movements. Before the French Revolution, Jews were not allowed to reside in the cities of Alsace. They lived in villages, often on the outskirts of the major cities.

My two grandparents, witnesses of that era, were from these small villages. They were born in this rural world, simple, far from the hustle and bustle of big cities. My maternal grandfather was born in Bolsenheim, and my grandmother in Muttersholz. Villages that whispered of the past, places where time seemed to flow differently.

The history of Alsace is intimately linked to that of Germany, and the German occupation of Alsace-Lorraine was a major turning point. Industrialization followed, radically transforming the social and economic landscape. Cities gained in importance, attracting many Jews from the surrounding villages. These population movements reflected deep changes in the life of Jewish communities.

The Jews from the villages, including my ancestors, often practiced modest trades, such as cattle or grain merchants, and even peddlers. Living in precarious economic conditions, they aspired to a better life. These stories, these journeys, shaped my family, leading us eventually to Strasbourg, where I was born, at the heart of an era of change and challenge.

In 1870, after the German conquest, my family faced a crucial choice. A part decided to leave Alsace for the United States to avoid German military service, while another preferred to settle in France. During this turbulent period, I had an uncle, born in 1852, who at 18 years old was a mobile guard in Strasbourg. He witnessed the dramatic events of the Prussian siege of 1870, including the great fire that devastated the city.

My grandmother, with her brothers and sisters, lived through these times of upheaval. One of her brothers settled in Remiremont in the Vosges. During the Dreyfus Affair, as a barber, he suffered the antisemitism of the garrison officers who broke the windows of his shop, forcing him to move to Nancy. Two other brothers emigrated to the United States, but regularly returned to visit the family.

My paternal grandfather is from Lindgolsheim, a small village near Strasbourg, and my paternal grandmother from Ritzels, near the German border. During World War I, my father, then a German soldier, bought a shoe store on Grand-Rue in Strasbourg, which he developed until the eve of the Second World War.

My parents were married in 1913. Shoemaking was my father's specialty. In my family, the trades were varied, but we were not yet in the era of academic professions. We were merchants and intermediaries. My father was mobilized in 1914, but, reluctant to risk his life for Emperor Wilhelm II, he found a way to be repatriated to Strasbourg, where he ended the war as a local garrison soldier.

During this time, my mother managed the shoe store. After the war, my father was able to develop the business. My parents worked hard after World War I to establish their trade. It was a favorable time for enterprising and hardworking people.

I was born in 1919, in an Alsace marked by the aftermath of World War I. Tragically, in 1920, my older sister, Suzanne, passed away from pneumonia, a merciless disease at that time. It was a huge shock for my mother, a pain that never left her. In 1922, my family grew with the birth of my little sister, Simone.

During my childhood, Strasbourg was the stage of my daily life, a city vibrant with culture and history. I had a classical education, crowned by studies at a business school. In 1936, my father sent me to Paris for an apprenticeship at Chaussures Heyraud, a formative experience that prepared me to join the family business.

Back in Strasbourg in 1937, I joined my father in managing the family store. Meanwhile, he had acquired another shop at Place Gutenberg. Our business was thriving, but the threat of war was already looming on the horizon.

Regarding national identity, the majority of Alsatian Jews, including my family, were resolutely pro-French. There was no marked sympathy for Germany, quite the contrary. This loyalty towards France was deeply rooted in our community, without ambivalence or conflict.

I remember a photo that I mentioned earlier, the one that illustrates my family's roots, testifying to our attachment to Alsatian soil and the French nation. Our identity was clear, our belonging unquestionable, even in the whirlwind of political changes and conflicts that shaped Alsace during these turbulent years.

My uncle David, residing in Nancy with my maternal grandparents since 1900, was naturally incorporated into the French army during World War I. His slight leg disability prevented him from going to the front, so he served in the rear-guard throughout the conflict.

As for my father, he served in the German army, in accordance with the military obligations imposed on Alsatians at the time. This never caused any family conflict. Despite his German uniform, my father, like many Alsatian Jews, was deeply pro-French. This loyalty to France was natural and never questioned.

My upbringing took place in a unique cultural mix. My mother tongue is French, but Alsatian, the dialect so characteristic of our region, was an important part of my linguistic identity. I was perfectly bilingual, oscillating between French and Alsatian with ease. German, though familiar, was not my language of choice.

At home, the coexistence of French and Alsatian was natural. My mother, having grown up in Nancy, spoke impeccable French, while my father, though less fluent, also communicated in French. Family conversations were a fluid mix of these two languages, without conscious effort. We never spoke German, as no one in the family really mastered it. This linguistic atmosphere was reflective of an Alsatian Judaism, rooted between two cultures but resolutely turned towards France.

I learned German at school, but it was distinct from my Jewish education, which I will now address. Judaism in Alsace was deeply traditional, rooted in practices and customs. However, it must be admitted that our level of Jewish culture and knowledge was rather limited. Members of our community knew how to read Hebrew, followed the prayers, and observed the laws of kashrut. But their understanding did not extend beyond these practices. This gap later contributed to a certain assimilation and an increase in intermarriages.

In my family, we followed Jewish traditions with a certain degree of flexibility. Although the store was open on Shabbat, my father, a heavy smoker, never smoked on that day. We also did not undertake trips on Shabbat. These were contradictions, certainly, but they reflected an undeniable attachment to traditions, which my parents managed to transmit to my sister and me.

We observed Jewish holidays, and Shabbat was celebrated traditionally, with visits to the synagogue. However, economic and social life imposed its constraints. For example, I went to class on

Shabbat, illustrating the mix of tradition and modernity that characterized our life.

Regarding secular education, there was no choice but public school. There was indeed a Jewish primary school in Strasbourg, but it did not meet the expectations of Jewish families wanting higher quality education. My sister and I attended the lyceum, both at primary and secondary levels, with non-Jewish classmates. This school experience was representative of our integration into general society while maintaining a connection to our Jewish heritage.

In the environment where we lived, interactions between Jews and non-Jews were frequent. Although there was antisemitism, it was not a major inconvenience in our daily life. We never encountered serious problems in this regard. I had non-Jewish friends, but our relationships had their limits.

In our home, close friendships were primarily with other Jewish families. With non-Jews, there was always a point beyond which the relationship did not progress. For example, in our building, there was a concierge, a wonderful woman whom my parents greatly appreciated. She had worked for my parents before her marriage and had maintained a strong bond with our family. She had a little girl, and at Christmas, we used to go to their Christmas tree to offer a small gift. However, our interactions were limited to these gestures of courtesy.

As for Jewish holidays, like Hanukkah, they were celebrated exclusively within our community. We did not invite non-Jews to these celebrations. This separation of social and cultural spheres reflected the reality of the time and of our community in Alsace. Our traditions and practices were preserved within our family and community circle while maintaining respectful coexistence with our non-Jewish neighbors.

In Strasbourg, the Jewish community life was very present and active. My sister and I attended Talmud Torah on Thursday and Sunday mornings, the school holidays. However, the education received there was quite basic. I remember my bar mitzvah in 1932, where I read three verses from the Sefer Torah without really understanding their meaning, due to a lack of in-depth explanations. At that time, my interest was probably more oriented towards the gifts associated with the event than the religious significance itself.

In parallel, there were very active Jewish youth movements in Strasbourg. The Jewish scouts, for example, were well established as early as the 1920s. There were also Zionist youth movements, active before, during, and especially after the First World War. The Keren Kayemet, in particular, enjoyed great activity. Almost all Jewish families had boxes to collect funds for Palestine, and most people were well informed about the situation there. However, our personal involvement in these movements did not extend beyond these basic community activities.

This dynamic reflected a certain commitment to our Jewish identity and the Zionist cause, but to a limited extent, focused on traditional practices and community support rather than active and in-depth participation in political or religious movements.

Although I was never involved in a youth movement, my sister joined the neutral girl scouts in Strasbourg. This distinction between "neutral", Catholic, Protestant, and Israelite was common in youth movements at that time, reflecting the cultural and religious diversity of the city.

Strasbourg, with its dynamic and active Jewish community, has always been a center of intense cultural and religious life. The city was a melting pot of traditions and innovations, where different faiths coexisted, each with its own organizations and activities. This vibrancy was particularly notable in the Jewish community, known for its commitment and vitality.

My sister, participating in the neutral girl scouts, benefited from an enriching experience, allowing her to immerse herself in a secular environment while remaining connected to our cultural and religious heritage. This participation reflected a balance between our Jewish identity and our integration into the broader Strasbourg society, a balance that characterized the lives of many Jewish families at that time.

One of the most significant events for the Jewish community in Strasbourg before the Second World War was undoubtedly the construction and inauguration of the large synagogue on Quai Kléber. This synagogue, an imposing and prestigious building, was inaugurated at the beginning of the 20th century, around 1901 or 1902, although the exact date escapes me. It represented a major turning point for our community, symbolizing both our prosperity and our integration into the city.

Before the construction of this grand synagogue, the Jewish community gathered in an older and more modest synagogue on Sainte-Hélène Street, located in the old quarter of Strasbourg. However, with the growth of the Jewish population, this space became too cramped. The new synagogue, erected in a developing neighborhood not far from the central market, quickly became a symbol of pride for all of us. Its visible and central location in the city testified to the presence and growing importance of the Jewish community in the life of Strasbourg.

It's important to note that, between 1870 and the First World War, Strasbourg saw the arrival of many German Jews. This immigration contributed to the cultural and religious enrichment of the local Jewish community, bringing new perspectives and traditions. The grand synagogue on Quai Kléber, with its majestic architecture, embodied this evolution, becoming a vital center for the religious, social, and cultural life of the Jews of Strasbourg.

German Judaism, known for its entrepreneurial spirit in the field of Jewish institutions, had a significant impact on the Jewish community of Strasbourg, especially during the period of German occupation. It was during this time that the main Jewish works in Strasbourg were founded, often thanks to the initiative and support of German Jewish families.

A significant clinic was established, as well as a school, called the "work school." This school played a similar role to that of ORT in later years. Orphanages, one for boys and another for girls, were also founded, as well as other more specific religious works. These institutions were largely supported by German families, who were generous and proactive in funding public works.

Among the notable achievements was also the Elisa Hospice, a retirement home founded in memory of a daughter of the Ratisbonne family. This family is particularly interesting: in the 19th century, one of the Ratisbonne brothers went to the Holy Land and converted to Christianity, founding the Order of the Sisters of Sion. Another brother, president of the Consistory in Strasbourg, created the Elisa Hospice in tribute to his daughter who died young. This hospice, which still exists today, has evolved significantly over the years.

These developments are a testament to the deep commitment of both local and German Jews to their community in Strasbourg. Their generosity and initiative played a crucial role in the creation of institutions that not only served the Jewish community but also enriched the social and cultural life of the city as a whole.

In Strasbourg, there was no strict separation between German and Alsatian Jews. They were part of what is called the Great Community or the Consistorial Community, and there was no notable distinction in their religious practice or social integration. The German Jews in Strasbourg were not in large numbers. They were mainly industrialists or people linked to power and had some influence.

Regarding the Jews of Eastern Europe, the Ostjuden, it is possible that they were also part of the community, but they were not distinct as a separate group within the Consistorial Community.

It is true that in Strasbourg, a community of strict observance formed very early. This occurred when the organ was introduced into the grand synagogue of Strasbourg. This phenomenon, where a group refused the introduction of the organ, was common in Germany and led to the creation of their own community, known as the Ost-Streitsgemeinde. This schism reflected differences in religious practice and the way of conceiving Judaism, rather than ethnic or national differences.

The Jewish community of Strasbourg was indeed diverse. In addition to the main Consistorial Community, there was a community of strict observance, as well as a community of Ostjuden that gradually developed. These different communities coexisted, each with its own practices and traditions, and there were three distinct minyanim, or prayer groups, in the city.

As for my family, we attended the historic synagogue on Quai Kléber. We lived in a neighborhood about 20 minutes away from this synagogue. In 1923, my parents had bought a building in this new neighborhood, and that's where we lived.

The approach of the Second World War would bring profound and devastating changes, not only for our family but also for the entire Jewish community of Strasbourg. This period marks a crucial turning point in our history, where our lives and our community would be tested in an unprecedented way.

From 1938, the tensions foreshadowing the Second World War were palpable, and the year 1939 was marked by increasingly worrying signs, such as the Anschluss and the invasion of Czechoslovakia. My parents, anticipating the upcoming troubles, had taken the precaution of renting furnished accommodation in the Vosges for vacations, while considering the possibility of using it as a refuge if necessary.

ChapTER 2

Setptember 1939. The evacuation order

When September 1, 1939, arrived, Strasbourg, along with other localities near the Rhine, was subjected to a forced evacuation. My father had already taken my mother, sister, and grandparents to this accommodation a few days earlier. My father and I followed during the official evacuation. We took with us what we could, trying to preserve our most precious or indispensable belongings as best as possible.

Thus, we found ourselves in Gérardmer, a place that was to serve as a temporary refuge in the face of the uncertainty and dangers of the imminent war. This period marked a heartbreaking turning point in our lives, distancing us from our home and plunging us into an uncertain future. Our family, like so many others, found itself confronted with the urgency of the situation, trying to maintain a semblance of normality in a rapidly and irreversibly changing world.

The order to evacuate Strasbourg came quite suddenly, but not totally unexpectedly, given the growing tensions in Europe. We were mainly informed by the radio, which was then our main source of information on external events. Additionally, the evacuation order was officially posted in the city, making the situation inevitably real and urgent.

The order stipulated that trains would be made available to residents to take them to host departments, particularly the Dordogne, with destinations like Périgueux, and the Haute-Vienne, with Limoges. However, my family chose a different path. My father owned a car, which allowed us to head to our accommodation in Gérardmer, where we had already sent my mother, sister, and grandparents.

I remember family discussions about what to take. These moments were filled with a certain urgency and anxiety. We had to quickly decide on essential items, leaving behind much of our belongings and our usual life. It was a difficult exercise of sorting, separating immediate necessities from possessions to which we were attached. Decisions had to be made quickly, as there was constant pressure of time and the rapidly evolving situation.

This forced evacuation was a moment of profound upheaval for our family, tearing us away from our familiar environment and projecting us into an uncertain future. It was a hasty goodbye to our home, our friends, and the life we knew, without knowing what the future held.

The evacuation of Strasbourg, a normally bustling city, was total and imperative. The instruction was clear: everyone had to leave, except for certain essential establishments like a few restaurants, medical points, and of course, the military troops. Only those with special authorization from the French military authorities were exempt from this directive. This measure, taken under the aegis of the French government, was a sign of the confidence placed in the Maginot Line. The inhabitants, including myself, were convinced of its effectiveness in protecting us from German offensives. This confidence was also supported by our faith in General Gamelin, the head of the French army. In our minds, the Maginot Line was an infallible bulwark, a guarantee of security in the heart of these uncertain times.

The purpose of the evacuation of Strasbourg was not only to protect military areas but also to take precautions to minimize civilian casualties in case of bombing. This measure was also intended to clear space for military maneuvers, avoiding the presence of civilians as an obstacle.

Faced with this situation, our family had to close the store. We took the key, leaving behind most of the goods. Only what we could carry in our car was saved. It was a poignant moment, marked by nostalgia and memories of my grandparents. My paternal grandmother had passed away in 1938, and my paternal grandfather, whom I had never known, had died much earlier, in 1905. These thoughts added an extra layer of emotion to our hasty departure from Strasbourg, a city on the brink of becoming a ghost of its former bustle.

The loss of my paternal grandmother in 1938 had left a painful imprint on our family. As for my maternal grandparents, they lived with my uncle, aunt, and cousin just below our apartment. When the evacuation order was given, they all had to leave, just like us. They managed to find accommodation in Gérardmer, a fallback town for many Strasbourgers during this troubled period.

My uncle, for his part, had been mobilized in the territorial forces, adding an extra layer of worry to our family situation. Despite the uncertainty and fear, we all headed to Gérardmer, carrying with us the keys to our homes and businesses, not left under a doormat but kept preciously in our pockets. This evacuation meant much more than a simple change of location; it was the beginning of a new era, full of uncertainties but also of family solidarity in adversity.

In Gérardmer, our settlement was relatively easy, despite the simplicity and harshness of the conditions. The town, known for its picturesque lake and idyllic holiday setting, offered many furnished accommodations, which was a considerable advantage for us and the many other refugees, especially those coming from Colmar and the surrounding areas.

This suddenly formed community of refugees included a significant portion of Jews, like us, seeking refuge far from their homes. The presence of a synagogue in Gérardmer was a source of comfort. It became a central point for our community life, offering a place of worship and gathering. Religious services, in particular, were important moments, reinforcing our sense of belonging and resilience in the face of adversity.

The experience in Gérardmer, though marked by the context of war and evacuation, was also a time of solidarity and sharing, where the community united to face the challenges of the moment.

This uprooting was a complex ordeal, mixing the uncertainty of the early days with the harsh reality of adaptation. At first, I thought it would be like a long vacation, a temporary change. But soon, material problems took precedence. We had to organize ourselves for basic needs, like food. We had kosher meat brought in from Colmar. It was one detail among many, but it symbolized this constant need for adaptation.

The winter in Gérardmer was particularly trying. Temperatures dropped to freezing levels, reaching minus 28 degrees, even minus 33 in Robirmont. Shutters froze on the windows, and toilets stopped functioning due to the frost. Every day was a struggle to keep warm, and splitting wood became a crucial routine for our survival.

Among these difficulties, a significant event was the death of my maternal grandmother at the end of October in Gérardmer. She was buried under a thick layer of snow. The memories of that day remain etched in my mind, evoking deep sadness. The grave could not be dug immediately because of the frozen ground. We had to wait for a slight thaw. Her death at 81 was accelerated by several minor ailments that worsened with age and this abrupt uprooting. It was a moment of deep sadness, mixed with the harsh reality of our situation.

These experiences, as painful as they were, shaped my view of life and resilience. The necessity to adapt to a hostile environment while bearing grief and loss is an invaluable life lesson.

In Gérardmer, my life took a different turn than I could have imagined. Having left high school to enter a business school, I had completed my studies at the end of 1935. So, upon our arrival in Gérardmer, I had no more school ties. This was a major change for me, moving from a structured and predictable environment to an uncertain existence in this small town.

We settled as best as we could in Gérardmer. My parents had always been frugal, living modestly but adequately. We lacked nothing essential but avoided any unnecessary expenses. This habit of saving proved crucial during the war. Without regular income, we depended on these savings to face the many difficulties. It was a time of restriction, but also of learning about the value of foresight and prudent resource management.

Each day brought its challenges, but thanks to my parents' frugality and foresight, we managed to overcome the most difficult moments. This experience taught me the importance of financial caution, a lesson I have kept throughout my life.

When we realized that our stay in Gérardmer would be prolonged, we decided to return to Strasbourg to retrieve essential belongings, both for us and for my grandparents. Initially, we transported our personal effects in my father's car. But soon, we also began to bring back goods from our store.

October, November, then December passed, and it became evident that leaving our stock of goods in Strasbourg was an unnecessary loss. We had a substantial stock, especially with the winter orders that had been largely profitable. We hadn't anticipated this situation; usually, to stop orders, it would have been necessary to plan six months in advance.

Faced with this unforeseen reality, we decided to sell this stock. It was a pragmatic measure, allowing us not to waste precious resources and to generate income in these uncertain times. It was a difficult but necessary task, reflecting our ability to adapt and face the challenges posed by the circumstances. Each return trip to Strasbourg was a reminder of our past life and a step towards managing our new reality.

The situation we faced was unprecedented. The two stores we had in Strasbourg were full of goods. Initially, we rented a quarter of a ballroom to store the shoes. This seemed like a temporary solution, but soon, we had to rent the entire hall in Gérardmer to accommodate our entire stock.

The trips between Strasbourg and Gérardmer became increasingly frequent. Faced with this necessity, the owner of the van we were using removed the seats to allow us to transport more goods. We packed the parcels of shoes ourselves, facing this task alone. Throughout the winter, we made numerous trips, although I cannot say exactly how many.

Once the merchandise was installed and sorted in the ballroom, we began to approach local shoe merchants to sell it. Our goal was clear: we could not keep this merchandise. Despite the difficulties, we managed to sell a good part of it, although it was not easy. At that time, the French industry was still functioning normally, and there were no major military operations. This period was called the "Phoney War," during which the German and French armies faced each other without really engaging.

While we waited, not knowing what exactly, our incomprehension grew. Yet, a blind trust in our military and police leaders persisted. It was spring, but the situation remained unchanged. My father and I spent our days driving around the region, looking for buyers for our goods. This incessant quest unknowingly transformed us into itinerant merchants. This was our new reality, dictated by circumstances, a role we had never imagined taking on.

In May 1940, with all the tensions and restrictions characteristic of that period, and despite the beginning of fuel shortages, our family still had vouchers allowing us to refuel. This spared us major difficulties. We drove cautiously, without excess, without waste. We only used the car for essential trips, aware of the necessity to conserve resources for more critical moments.

My parents were particularly foresighted. They followed an old tradition, widespread among Jewish families, of keeping a little gold aside. Gold is a safe-haven asset, offering a certain security in times of economic or social upheaval. This gold, they neither wanted to sell nor use immediately. They viewed the future with caution, and with the war rumbling, they decided to take measures to preserve it.

Thus, they rented a safety deposit box in a bank in Orléans. This choice was not arbitrary. Orléans was a strategic city, more set back from the emerging front line in the north. If the situation were to worsen and we were forced to leave our home, Orléans appeared as a judicious choice for potential retreat. It was a fairly central position in the Hexagon and offered us peace of mind in the face of uncertain times.

In short, this period was marked by the need to plan ahead, to think in advance about precautionary measures to face what the future held. It was this foresight of my parents that allowed us to go through these difficult times with a bit more serenity.

I distinctly remember that morning, May 10, 1940, when my father and I set out for Orléans. Midway, we found ourselves in the Langres region, faced with a total halt in traffic. The air was heavy with the sound of bombs exploding, an unmistakable sign of the German offensive that had started that day.

The surprise was total. Columns of smoke rose here and there, testifying to the impact of the bombs. Enemy planes were everywhere, and we could hear the characteristic whistling of Stukas diving on their targets. After what seemed an interminable time, the assaults ceased, and we were able to continue our journey.

In Orléans, the mission was accomplished quickly: a night spent in the city, renting a safety deposit box at the bank, and then returning to Gérardmer. The initial plan might have seemed simple, but events took a dramatically faster turn than expected. The Germans were advancing at an incredible speed. Everyone hoped that the Marne would be the scene of a new miracle, as in 1914, but there was no miracle this time.

Chapter 3

June 1940. The enlistment

During this time, the army called me up. My contingent was actually scheduled to be mobilized in October 1939, but this was postponed due to a lack of equipment. Finally, I was called to serve on June 8, 1940, in the 184th Artillery Regiment in Valence.

Events accelerated rapidly. Paris fell on June 14, and it was on that day my parents, along with my elderly grandfather, took the road of the Exodus. A tragically common story among so many French people, fleeing in front of the advancing enemy. When the fuel eventually ran out, they found themselves in the Cantal, in Albepierre, where they took refuge in the barn of a certain Madame Jacomi, among the straw.

Back in Valence, I was introduced to military discipline and trained in handling the 75mm cannon, then considered the pinnacle of military progress. Then came General de Gaulle's appeal on June 18, urging us to continue the fight from England. This was unthinkable for us: France capitulating to Germany? Yet, a few days later, the armistice was signed. Marshal Pétain took the head of the government, and the France we knew began to fade before our eyes.

Personally, I did not hear General de Gaulle's appeal. In the barracks, it was unthinkable that this call, considered seditious at the time, would be broadcast. We only learned of this event through discussions and exchanges among comrades. Some of us had ventured into town, and that's how we learned that a certain Colonel de Gaulle had taken to the airwaves from London, calling all French people to join him to continue the fight for France, but from abroad.

Around June 18, this new option, that of resistance beyond borders, began to be known among us. However, we had been so accustomed to trusting the French army and the government that we did not immediately grasp the full extent of the disaster that had actually occurred. It was a vision distorted by trust and disbelief, but the facts were there: the French army was suffering heavy losses, and many soldiers were being captured by the enemy, including three of my cousins, the sons of one of my father's sisters.

It was only later that I became fully aware of the magnitude of the events, regarding the army, the prisoners, or the situation of my own family.

Back at the Valence barracks, one day, we received the order to prepare to move south. Our unit was loaded into cattle wagons. The collective hope, our hope, was that we were being taken to North Africa. There, we thought we would have the opportunity to join the fighting forces and resume combat. This idea dominated among the soldiers, that of a continuation of the struggle, even if the mainland fell into German hands.

After the armistice signed on June 22, 1940, the situation for Jews in France became particularly precarious. Like many other Jews at the time, my family and I perceived the defeat not just as a loss of our French identity. It was also the announcement of an imminent danger to our very existence. The news of what was happening in Germany with the subjugation of Jews, the concentration camps, arbitrary arrests, and assaults was well known to us. This reality was alarming, and with France's defeat, the illusion that the nation could still protect us quickly dissipated.

Marshal Pétain, meanwhile, was a well-known and once respected figure, the "victor of Verdun," an emblematic character of World War I. Before the war, it would have been hard for anyone to suspect him of collaborating with the Germans. But, history quickly showed how naive this trust in him was. Once in power, he established the Vichy regime, which collaborated with the Nazi occupiers.

In my family, and generally among the Jewish community, there was no sympathy for Pétain or his policies. De Gaulle's call did not necessarily immediately influence everyone, given its initially limited reach. Nevertheless, for Jews and many other French people who valued freedom and resistance, this call was a glimmer of hope, albeit distant and uncertain at this stage.

The armistice signed between Pétain and the Germans was not just a military compromise; it was also the prelude to a dark period for the Jews. The growing feeling was that the Germans were not only the enemies of France but were also our direct oppressors. With the experience of German refugees arriving in France, we knew what was happening, and we already had a terrible understanding of what a Nazi regime could mean. We didn't yet know the full extent, but we already knew that for us, Jews, it was a cataclysm.

Indeed, I did not trust Marshal Pétain from the start. Among the general Jewish community, there was quite a widespread instinctive mistrust, though of course, there might have been exceptions. But overall, we were aware of the dangers posed by the new direction of the government in

the face of Nazi occupation.

During our move south, the fleeting hope of escaping to join the Free Forces quickly collapsed. The train did not take us to a port but to a camp in Barcarès, where we were dropped off. This camp had previously hosted Republican Spanish refugees after Franco's victory. There, conditions were more than basic: wooden barracks set up on sand, and fleas were everywhere.

We spent a few weeks there under the crushing sun, typical of the Mediterranean region. The conditions were difficult, and Barcarès was far from being a place of convalescence. After this stay, we were transferred to a village near Perpignan, where we slept in barns. It was a slight improvement, considering it was summer and temperatures could be very high.

Our days were monotonously uneventful. The main occupation seemed to be killing fleas, a daily battle, while the rest of the time, there was practically nothing to do. The inactivity and lack of a clear perspective for the future contributed to a general feeling of abandonment and uncertainty about what the future held for us.

We were stationed, and daily life in the camp was marked by deep boredom and a palpable lack of activity. Apart from the imperative of keeping the barracks clean and fighting flea infestations, there were no tasks or military exercises. No training, nothing that resembled preparation for combat. It was a period of great emptiness.

When we were moved to the small village of Pia, near Perpignan, our living conditions slightly improved. We were housed with locals, which allowed us to better supply ourselves with fresh products like vegetables and eggs. We could finally breathe a bit, relax after the closeness of the Barcarès camp.

In Pia, I managed to reestablish contact with my family. I had a cousin in Perpignan, and through another cousin in Bordeaux, I finally obtained my parents' address in the Cantal. We exchanged a few postcards that are still dear to me. My parents had moved from Madame Jacomis's barn to the Hôtel de la Croix-Blanche in Murat, the capital of the region.

Unfortunately, it was there that my grandfather passed away, in July 1940, at the hospital in Murat. He was buried in the town cemetery. My parents, meanwhile, had learned of the presence in Montpellier of a family friend from Strasbourg, the Vinter family, who had also left Alsace to flee the invader.

This network of contacts between families and friends, refugees scattered across the country, was essential for maintaining some semblance of coherence in our lives disrupted by the war. It allowed us to keep connections, exchange news, and support each other through these difficult times.

After the time spent in the small village near Perpignan, my parents decided to go to Montpellier. They had no particular preferences for any place, no attachments elsewhere, just the knowledge of friends' presence there. Once there, they rented a furnished apartment and settled in.

As for me, from Pia, our group was transferred to Fort Mont-Louis in the Pyrénées-Orientales. This fort, built in the 17th century, is located at an altitude of 1800 meters. The conditions were harsh, but the air was fresh, and we had a kind of small mountain cure for two weeks, despite the absence of military activities. Without personal weapons, there was not even a guard duty to perform.

It was at this time that I received my parents' contact in Montpellier thanks to the address provided by my cousin. Establishing communication with them was a small comfort in these uncertain times.

Later, from Mont-Louis, we were redeployed further north, in an arid mountainous region of the Massif Central, near Lodève, with the goal of creating elements of the Chantiers de Jeunesse. Indeed, after the armistice, the French army had been largely dissolved, except for a small armistice army composed mainly of career military personnel. Soldiers who had not been captured had been released, except for those, like me, who were to perform their military service.

ChapTER 4

Les Chantiers de Jeunesse – The Youth Work Camps

The Chantiers de Jeunesse (Youth Work Camps) were designed to replace the mandatory military service for young French men and to instill values of work, camaraderie, and discipline, in the spirit of the new Vichy regime. This was a period of transition and adaptation to a France transformed by defeat and armistice, seeking its way under the weight of German presence and a collaborating government.

My group, the class of 1939, 4th quarter, was transformed into the Chantiers de Jeunesse. These camps aimed to prepare the youth to become the face of the new France according to Vichy ideals: "work, family, homeland". They were meant to be a return to nature and fundamental values.

We were supposed to participate in physical work, such as tree cutting and installing water supply systems, to prepare a camp for our future residence and possibly for other activities.

Arriving in August, we were assigned tents and started clearing the land. We had to remove vegetation and prepare the soil for our permanent tent sites or log cabins, which we were tasked to build ourselves. At the same time, it was necessary to set up a central space for gatherings, with a flagpole.

Each group tackled its tasks. Some were more skilled than others, bringing their professional skills acquired before the call-up, like farmers or craftsmen. Personally, I was less useful in terms of manual skills, having no experience as a lumberjack or carpenter. So I found myself more in a support role, carrying materials, digging the earth among other tasks. Fortunately, we had more experienced companions, including people from the same village in Lorraine as me.

We lived in tents until December. Afterward, we were delivered prefabricated barracks. We contributed to assembling them, and it was around this central ground that we settled in these structures once winter came. This marked a certain progression in our living conditions after months spent in more austere precarity.

In the Chantiers de Jeunesse where I was assigned, conditions were rudimentary; without running water or electricity, the facilities were basic. We washed in the stream, and as winter approached, the water froze, making the task even more arduous and uninviting. This cold was enough to deter most of us from attempting this experience each morning.

However, despite these primitive conditions, we were spared from serious illnesses. There was an effort to maintain hygiene at an acceptable level. For example, we were vaccinated against diphtheria and other infectious diseases with the TAB vaccine (triple anti-bacillary), commonly administered to 20-year-olds in France.

As for the camp's administration, it was overseen by military officers, with a minimum of discipline instated. The camp leader was a lieutenant, assisted by sub-lieutenants or aspirants. These men were generally friendly and not at all indoctrinated by Vichy ideology, some even openly hostile to Pétain.

I remember, when leaving, the camp leader, knowing my Jewish status, offered his help if I needed it in the future — a proposition that meant a lot, especially in these uncertain times. Although I never had to call on him, his offer remains in my memory as a gesture of solidarity.

The Chantiers de Jeunesse were meant to embody one of the central elements of the National Revolution advocated by Vichy, intended to train and educate the new French youth. In theory, it was about bringing these young people closer to the land and work, but the practical realities and daily difficulties, as well as the attitudes of the camp officials, often overshadowed these theoretical objectives.

Indeed, during the first months following the French defeat in 1940, the Vichy regime was still establishing its policies and programs. As for our experience in the Chantiers de Jeunesse at that time, the focus was on managing immediate and practical concerns such as setting up the camp, installing water supply, and other essential infrastructures.

Political indoctrination activities, if they were planned to become a component of the program, were not yet implemented or at least not perceptibly for us. It was just the beginning of the National Revolution, and infrastructure and organization were more pressing priorities.

As for the status of Jews, which was enacted in October 1940, the echo of this discriminatory legislation did not immediately resonate in the daily life of our camp. We were busy with physical work and communal living, and weekend passes allowed me to be with my family, offering an escape from political problems and an opportunity to discuss the situation with my parents.

To join my family in Montpellier on weekends, I had to find a truck going to Lodève and then take a small mountain train. It was a fortunate coincidence to be geographically close to my parents. These reunions were precious, not only for practical matters like laundry and supplies, but especially for the moral support and information they could give me about the evolving situation for the Jewish community.

During the period that included the Jewish High Holidays of Rosh Hashanah and Yom Kippur in September 1940, I was able to obtain permits that allowed me to join Montpellier and participate in the celebrations organized in the city. A large warehouse was made available by a businessman, Elie Cohen, who stood out for his exceptional generosity. He offered his fabric warehouse so that the community of Jewish refugees could gather and pray.

The organization of these gatherings was led by the military chaplain and Rabbi, Henri Schilli, whose leadership and words had a significant and lasting influence on me, although I did not have the opportunity to engage further with him at the time. The presence and atmosphere of these moments shared with the Jewish community left a strong imprint on my consciousness.

My parents, settled in a furnished house on rue du Pont Juvenal near the Montpellier train station, were part of a large community of refugees that included families from different regions, such as Saint-Dié and Luxembourg. This house had about twenty apartments and had become a rallying point for these families seeking a sanctuary amidst the turmoil of the war.

Community life in Montpellier was rich, and mutual support was central. It was in this community that I integrated after my release from the Chantiers de Jeunesse in early 1941. This marked a new chapter in my life, a time when I could become more deeply involved in local Jewish life and witness firsthand the effects of Vichy's anti-Semitic policies on the refugee community.

When I returned to Montpellier in February 1941, the community of Jewish refugees faced the new realities imposed by the Vichy regime through the Statut des Juifs. For many, as recent refugees not yet professionally integrated in the region, these measures did not have as direct an impact as on more established professions like teachers or civil servants.

However, one of the most palpable consequences of the Statut des Juifs was the introduction of the numerus clausus in universities, restricting higher education access for many Jewish students. This discriminatory element created difficulties for those wishing to undertake or continue their studies and represented a part of the future of the Jewish community.

Despite these constraints, the resilience of Montpellier's Jewish community was evident. The Winter family, for example, who had a fabric business in Strasbourg, managed to reopen a business and strived to maintain some economic stability while offering significant support to Jewish refugees. Their house became a gathering point and a place of comfort for many.

The Éclaireurs Israélites (Jewish Scouts) movement continued to play a key role for the city's Jewish youth, with Raymond Winter and my sister Simone involved in leading the scouts and guides groups. Simultaneously, the Jewish Youth of Montpellier (JGM), led by André Blum, also a refugee, reflected the determination of young people despite the restrictions imposed by the numerus clausus. André Blum himself had managed to enroll in medicine at the University of Montpellier.

In this challenging context, adaptability and community support were essential to mitigate the impacts of anti-Semitic policies and to maintain a lasting social and cultural connection within the refugee Jewish population.

Upon demobilization from the Chantiers de Jeunesse in January, there was no particular celebration or honor for me. I was simply given a release certificate and wished good luck for the future. I remember the words of the lieutenant who had expressed his personal support and offered his help if I ever needed it. It was a gesture meant for me from him as an individual, not representative of an institution or a general sentiment.

Regarding anti-Semitism, I did not experience specific hostility or open discrimination within the Chantiers. To my knowledge, I was the only Jew in my section of approximately 120 people.

Back in Montpellier, the question arose of what path to take, especially in the limited context of opportunities that presented themselves. The situation was complex, with uncertain professional and personal horizons under the Vichy regime, particularly for a young Jew like myself.

CHAPTER 5

Organizing under Vichy

After leaving the Chantiers de Jeunesse in early 1941, I faced an uncertain future. Without a baccalaureate, access to higher education was barred for me anyway, and the restrictions imposed by the Vichy regime would have made university entrance improbable for a Jew like me.

The era was troubled, marked by news of the war in North Africa and Syria. The clashes around Benghazi, with their offensives and counter-offensives, captivated our attention, and we tried to follow the conflict's progress with the available means of information, despite censorship.

We clandestinely listened to the broadcasts from London and Free France, which were strictly forbidden by the Vichy government. Despite the danger, in our circle, listening to these bulletins at 9 p.m. had become a routine, a sacred moment where we stayed informed. These broadcasts brought us news from the outside world and represented moral support, a connection to the forces fighting against the Nazi occupation.

However, optimism was tempered by the reality of the situation. We were aware that the Germans were far from being in retreat; on the contrary, their offensive against England continued vigorously. The newspapers, controlled by the Vichy authorities, relayed this propaganda, and we had to read between the lines to try to understand what was really happening.

In this context, despite the uncertainty, we tried to hold on, to find ways to continue our lives while hoping for a favorable outcome to this dark period in history.

The information we received from the radio, while offering a glimpse of the outside and some comfort, was not always enough to counterbalance the omnipresence of the war and its consequences on our daily lives. We knew that the stakes were considerable and that the outcome of the war would be decisive for our future.

Our days were mainly focused on managing basic needs and the restrictions imposed by the occupier and the Vichy regime. Our primary concern was the quest for food: the long queues to get vegetables and other goods, obtaining bread tickets, and lining up for milk took up a significant part of our time.

Despite this heavy context, we looked to the future with hope, thanks to prospects of emigration. An uncle, my grandmother's brother living in the United States, was willing to send us affidavits, necessary documents to enter American territory. Thus, my parents began to seriously consider the option of emigration. In anticipation, I dedicated myself to learning English to prepare for a potential new life away from war and persecution, in hope of regained security and stability.

Learning English became one of my main objectives, both for my personal development and in view of emigrating to the United States, which emerged as a potential path to freedom. My father and I made several trips to Marseille to visit the American consulate in hopes of advancing our immigration case, taking advantage of the fact that the United States had not yet entered the war and a consulate was still operational on French soil.

However, obtaining the necessary affidavits and visas proved to be an arduous journey. Administrative procedures were considerably slowed down by high demand and bureaucratic processes. The queues were long, and it was not uncommon to have to return another day when our turn came too late and the consulate closed its doors.

This process stretched throughout 1941 and 1942, and unfortunately, when the affidavits finally arrived, it was already too late. On November 8, 1942, the Germans invaded the free zone of France, and movement restrictions intensified, making emigration impossible. All our hopes and efforts to leave France vanished in the face of the

German troops' advance, and no one could leave the country anymore, visa or not. Everything we had worked for turned out to be in vain.

Language learning became a positive and lasting aspect of this period of uncertainty. Even though our plans to emigrate to the United States were aborted, the English I learned then stayed with me. With changing hopes and delayed visas, I also added Spanish to my learning, fostering a new escape strategy: to illegally pass through Spain to reach England and join General de Gaulle's Free French Forces. I even began teaching Spanish to a few students, allowing me to share my newfound language skills.

ChapTER 6

Deepening my Judaism

This period was also marked by an expansion of my understanding of Judaism. In Montpellier, I discovered an active Sephardic community that practiced worship in a small office, adapted to their size throughout the year. This intimate setting offered a place where a harmonious compromise between Sephardic and Ashkenazi Jews, the latter being newcomers, allowed serene coexistence.

During major Jewish holidays, Sephardic celebrations were distinct, in accordance with their traditions. They had their own office that catered to their specific needs. Discovering another way of living Judaism than the one I knew in Alsace or Strasbourg enriched my view of religion and Jewish culture, adding a new dimension to my identity as a Jew.

For several months, I continued these language courses vigorously. I was also fortunate to receive instruction from a Jew of Polish origin who imparted a deep knowledge of Hebrew grammar and the Hebrew language itself. Friends of my age who shared these interests and enthusiasm for learning joined me, and together, we developed some fluency and an ear for the Hebrew language, which proved crucial for my future ability to understand and express myself in this language.

This period of intense linguistic learning was not just an acquisition of educational skills; it also represented a real rediscovery and affirmation of my Jewish identity. This was set against a backdrop where identity issues were intrinsically linked to historical events and a growing collective consciousness among Jews worldwide.

Whether this was a Zionist orientation or simply a rediscovery of Jewish identity is difficult to untangle, as these notions tend to overlap, especially in the context of the time. Learning Hebrew took on a symbolic and practical dimension, both as a means to connect to a millennia-old history and culture, and potentially as preparation for future use of the language in a Zionist context, should the opportunity or necessity for Aliyah (emigration to Jewish Palestine, later Israel) arise.

This period was marked by a true revelation: I was discovering another face of Judaism, far from the one I had known during my early childhood. I met Jews from Paris of Polish origin and especially Sephardic Jews from the old community of Montpellier, most of them originally from Salonica (Thessaloniki), Greece.

When I say "Sephardic," I must clarify that this term does not refer here to North African Jews, though it is commonly used in that sense. The Sephardim I'm talking about came from a very specific current in Jewish history, connected to the Ottoman Empire and the cultural exchanges of the Mediterranean world.

One figure who particularly caught my attention was Elie Cohen, a prosperous merchant from Montpellier. Like many other members of this Sephardic community, he had benefited from the education provided by the Alliance Israélite Universelle, a French organization that had established a network of schools for Jews in the East. Thus, despite their Eastern origins, these Jews were perfectly Francophone and fully integrated into local French life.

Confronting these different facets of Judaism, I realized how my experience of Jewish life as an Alsatian Jew was both specific and limited. Our lives were mainly centered around our integration as French Jews in a particular region of France. On the Yiddish spoken at home or during community gatherings, on the specific traditions and rituals practiced during religious holidays.

In contrast, the Jewish life of Eastern European Jews seemed much more rooted in a global Jewish consciousness, more independent of the national or regional context. Their Jewish identity was at the heart of their existence, not just one component among others.

I met fascinating personalities among them, like the magistrate Gnoun, who had lost his job following the application of the Statut des Juifs, or President Uziel, a typically Sephardic name from Salonica.

But more than a cultural shock, this encounter with other forms of Judaism was also a spiritual and intellectual awakening for me. For the first time, I became aware of the extent of my own ignorance about Judaism. This sparked in me a deep desire to learn and delve deeper into Jewish history and culture.

Rabbi Schilli, with his patience and openness, stirred this desire to learn within me. This marked a turning point in my journey, a time when I began to open up to much broader horizons.

Every Saturday night, we gathered with the Jewish Youth group of Montpellier, and on Sundays, we went out for group outings. We took turns presenting on various topics. I was asked to do a presentation on Maimonides. I consulted the library and found Munk's book on Maimonides, a work in French from the last century. Preparing this presentation, though very clumsy and basic, allowed me to discover Maimonides and open up to a whole other aspect of Judaism.

Of course, we also discussed Palestine, Zionism, and a range of other topics related to the Jewish world. This helped us broaden our horizons and better understand the scope and complexity of the Jewish experience.

CHAPTER 7

Learning to make shoes

During this time, I was also becoming more involved with a group of young Zionists in Montpellier. However, the Jewish Youth of Montpellier brought together a variety of tendencies and constituted a microcosm of Jewish diversity. These years were fundamental in forming the basis of my Jewish consciousness and fueling my desire to learn more about Jewish culture and history.

Each group had its own specific activities, but they also participated in the activities of the Jewish Youth of Montpellier. This created a form of unity, which was extremely positive. However, it wasn't enough to clarify the direction my future should take.

With the advice and agreement of my parents, I decided to join the professional school of Romand, in the Drôme, to learn manual shoe manufacturing. Given the inability of Jews to access studies or commerce due to the restrictions imposed by the Statut des Juifs, it seemed necessary to find a way to earn a living. No one knew how long the war would last, nor how long the Statut des Juifs would be in effect. Therefore, it was important to prepare for the future and develop skills and know-how that would be useful regardless of the circumstances.

Thus, this solution was finally adopted. On January 1, 1942, I left for Romans, in the Drôme. My cousin Hubert Hallel's family was then residing in Montélimar. After leaving Gérardmer following the debacle, they had stayed a few months in Paris before settling in Montélimar.

For six months, we learned to make shoes by hand, that is, the art of shoemaking, with waxed thread and making shoes from pieces of leather.

In the summer of 1942, I made contact with a shoe factory in La Tour-du-Pin, which had been a supplier to my father, to see if I could do a two-month internship in their company. My intention was then to continue my shoemaking training at the school in Nîmes.

In Nîmes, close to Montpellier, I began an important chapter of my life: my apprenticeship in the art of shoemaking. It was a professional school with a machine manufacturing workshop. I chose this place to learn about machines, a factory located in La Tour-du-Pin, in Isère. In the summer of 1942, I spent two months there, a crucial and formative period.

There, I didn't make finished shoes but rather drafts and prototypes. My days were devoted to learning the basics: cutting soles precisely with a cutting knife, meticulously preparing the groove for the stitch, making holes with the punch for the passage of the waxed thread. Each gesture was a fundamental learning experience, endowing me with valuable artisanal know-how.

Although this apprenticeship was extremely enriching, I often questioned where this path would lead. Was it an end in itself or simply a step towards something bigger? Despite these questions, I knew deep down that these skills, these moments spent shaping shoe drafts, would forge a part of my identity and my journey.

It was the summer of 1942. At that time, the first roundups of foreigners had begun in France. We were directly concerned. When I returned to Montpellier at the end of August 1942, these roundups had already taken place. Many Jews had been arrested, although some had managed to hide. I particularly remember a trip to the concentration camp, or rather the assembly camp in Agde, about thirty to forty kilometers from Montpellier. We had been asked to collect food from our community members - biscuits, dried fruits, chocolate, whatever was possible - to bring to the internees at the Agde camp.

Rabbi Schilly had organized, for a few young people and me, a visit to the internees at the Agde camp. One of the most striking images from this visit, which I will never forget, was that of a train ready to leave for Drancy. At the door of a wagon, a man I recognized from the services in Montpellier stood wrapped in his Talit, with Tefillin on his head, deep in prayer. This image is etched in my memory.

We distributed the food we had brought. At that time, we were still unaware of the "Final Solution," but we knew that the fate awaiting those taken away would not be enviable. We did not know who would return or in what state the survivors would come back.

Our actions, such as collections and visits to the Agde camp, were not limited to the context of the Grand Raffle. They were part of a broader effort, involving various organizations and individuals. Activities in camps like Agde, Rivesaltes, and Gurs were organized by several entities, notably OSE (Œuvre de Secours aux Enfants) and other dedicated aid organizations. Among the prominent figures, there were the camp chaplaincy, Chief Rabbi Hirschler, who was deported, and Chief Rabbi Schilli, both very active in this
work.

As for our study group in Montpellier, we were not involved as a formal group. There was no strict compartmentalization in our actions; when a need arose, everyone who could help was called upon. Thus, those who were available and willing to participate did so, without distinction of belonging to one group or another.

I did not personally meet escapees from the Agde or Gurs camps. Generally, those who managed to escape from these camps were immediately hidden in places far from the cities for security reasons.

A key player in liberating people from the camps was Rabbi Richelieu. He had influential contacts, notably through his acquaintance with a certain Camille Ernst, the secretary-general of the Montpellier prefecture. Ernst, a man of remarkable dedication, played a crucial role in obtaining many releases from these camps, which fell under his administrative jurisdiction. Thanks to his efforts, many people, especially Jews, were able to be released and owe him their lives.

His exceptional contribution was recognized in 1972 when he was honored at Yad Vashem, the Holocaust Memorial in Jerusalem, with the Righteous Among the Nations medal for his invaluable aid and courage.

I was aware that the roundups mainly targeted foreign Jews, but the situation concerned all of us. In Montpellier, many foreign Jews were hidden. My first involvement in clandestine activities dates back to September 1942, when I began bringing food to hidden Jews.

CHAPTER 8

Beginning of clandestine activities

During this time, clandestine activities were just beginning to get organized. Raymond Winter, the head of the Éclaireurs Israélites (Jewish Scouts), was already involved in providing false identity cards for those in hiding. This marked the beginning of such activities in our area.

These efforts were part of the 6th branch of the Éclaireurs Israélites, which was part of the broader structure of Jewish organizations. The 6th branch was responsible for education and nominally served as a cover for the Éclaireurs Israélites' clandestine activities. These activities were crucial in helping and protecting those endangered by the policies of the time.

The "sixième" (sixth) was part of the Éclaireurs Israélites and was a resistance organization created and led by them. In addition to their resistance activities, the Éclaireurs Israélites managed a network of farm schools aimed at providing education, a feature often mentioned in the literature about this period.

Regarding the distribution of food or aid to hidden refugees, my role involved collecting food containers prepared at a specific location and then carrying them to the hiding places of Jews in flight. I also had to convey messages or requests from those managing these hideouts. This work was an essential part of the aid provided to those in hiding, enabling them to remain out of sight while receiving the necessary support to survive in these challenging times.

I had specific addresses to deliver to. The number of people I was providing food to wasn't very high; personally, I was responsible for three people to whom I brought food for a few days before my departure to Nîmes. Then, I passed my responsibilities on to another person who took over.

There was a central organization, whose details I don't recall, responsible for sourcing the necessary ingredients, preparing meals, and making them ready for distribution. My role was simply to collect these prepared meals and bring them to the hidden individuals.

For my part, I left for Nîmes in early October to join the shoemaking school. This marked a turning point in my commitment during this period.

In Nîmes, where I went next, the school year had already started. My experience there was a new step in my journey during this period.

November 8, 1942, marks a crucial turning point: the Allied landing in North Africa. Following this event, the Germans invaded the southern zone of France, which until then had offered relative protection to French Jews. This invasion changed the situation, putting us directly in danger due to the German presence and the Gestapo.

Faced with this new threat, I immediately left Nîmes to return to Montpellier. There, an urgent question arose: what to do now? The conclusion was that we had to try to flee to Spain before the Germans reached the border. Raymond Winter, whom I mentioned earlier, knew a smuggler who could help us.

So, on the morning of November 8, I returned to Montpellier, and only three hours later, we were already on a train to Perpignan, ready to attempt our passage to Spain, seeking to escape German occupation.

Raymond Winter, André Blum (a medical student), myself, and one or two other youths whose names escape me, formed a small group in this escape attempt. Unfortunately, our arrival in Perpignan coincided with the arrival of the German troops. The smuggler, whose address Raymond Winter had, was nowhere to be found.

Faced with this delicate situation and the uncertainty of finding another reliable and safe smuggler, we decided not to pursue our attempt to cross into Spain. We chose to return to Montpellier, accepting this failure.

This escape attempt was a completely private initiative, not linked to any organization or movement. Anecdotally, during our short stay in Perpignan, we visited my cousins who still lived there. We had the opportunity to share a small evening meal with them and refresh ourselves before taking the night train back to Nîmes. It was a moment of respite in a period marked by uncertainty and danger.

Indeed, during our stay in Perpignan, we did not attempt other steps to find a smuggler. We lacked information and contacts on-site. Moreover, being strangers to Perpignan, we did not have local knowledge that could assist us. I even asked my cousin if he knew someone, but he could not help us.

It was essential to have a reliable address and safety guarantees. Without them, the risk was too high to fall into the hands of unscrupulous people who could deliver us directly to the police. Unfortunately, many attempts to cross into Spain resulted in arrests, imprisonments, or transfers to the Drancy camp, often after being tortured.

In this context, our decision not to continue our attempt and to return to Montpellier, then Nîmes, though sad, was probably the wisest. The situation was extremely perilous, and it was crucial not to act hastily

The experience of French Jewish prisoners of war in Germany during World War II is indeed remarkable and somewhat inexplicable. Despite being Jewish and held in prisoner-of-war camps in Germany, they survived the five years of the Hitler regime without facing specific persecution as Jews. This contrasts sharply with the tragic fate of the majority of Jews under the Nazi regime and is considered by many as a miraculous anomaly in a period marked by brutal persecution of Jews. The reason why these Jewish soldiers were spared from specific persecution remains largely unexplained, adding a layer of mystery to this dark period in history.

Among these Jewish prisoners of war were three of my cousins, brothers. One of them was fortunate enough to be repatriated in 1942 and reunited with his family, while the other two remained captives until the end of the war. These prisoners could receive parcels from their families, a crucial support during their captivity.

In 1942, Jews were also required to have their identity cards stamped with a "Juif" (Jew) marking. Due to a shortage of official stamps, some places used handwritten inscriptions, as seen on my own identity card. This measure was another manifestation of the systematic horror and discrimination Jews had to endure during this time.

My life in Nîmes during the early winter of 1942 revolved around several activities, including my apprenticeship at the shoemaking school and active participation in the youth movement. This period in Nîmes represented a time of personal growth and engagement in my studies and Jewish community life.

In Montpellier, before Nîmes, we had an outstanding cantor, Mr. Roth, from the small community of Insvillers in Alsace. He played a vital role in our community, particularly in teaching tefilah (prayer) to a group of young people, including me. Mr. Roth's teachings were not just about reciting prayers; they involved a deeper understanding of their meaning and role in our religious practice.

When I had to have the "Juif" stamp added to my identity card, I remember feeling deeply uncomfortable. Reacting quickly, I declared my card lost and obtained a new one without the "Juif" stamp. This new card became my main identification document, and I never used or showed the stamped one. This strategy was a way to navigate a context where stigmatization and dangers were omnipresent for Jews.

During the winter in Nîmes, despite the German presence and imposed curfews, life went on relatively calmly. A significant element of this period was the presence of Chief Rabbi Ernest Weil of Réguisheim. In his large apartment, he organized morning prayers (tefila), which my cousin Hubert and I regularly attended. These gatherings were special, uniting Jews of various origins, and represented a time when the Jewish community, despite challenging circumstances, found ways to come together and maintain its traditions and practices.

I had learned to read certain parts of the Torah, and among the youth, we organized a tefila (prayer service) for Shabbat afternoons. These gatherings allowed me to apply the knowledge I had acquired. It was important to me because it enabled me to contribute to the religious life of our community and strengthen my connection to my faith and culture during these uncertain times.

Regarding the concept of "hazara b'tchouva" (return to the faith), I wouldn't classify my experience in Nîmes as hazara b'tchouva in the strict sense. Instead, I saw it as a process of gaining knowledge that naturally led to an evolution in my practice and behavior. This process was more than just acquiring theoretical knowledge; it involved the practical application of what I learned, affecting how I lived my faith daily, although I did not observe all the mitzvot (commandments). It was a gradual path toward greater observance and a deeper understanding of my religion and its practices.

In this sense, what I experienced was an accession to religious knowledge, accompanied by increasing commitment to Jewish practices and traditions. It was a personal journey toward deeper and more engaged religious practice, influenced by the circumstances and environment of the time.

In the spring of 1943, I faced a delicate mission. Jean-Jacques Rhein, the head of the 6th section in Nîmes, approached me for a particular task. It involved escorting two young people, a boy and a girl, who were foreigners to our country and spoke very little French. They had received false papers certifying a non-Jewish identity. This precaution had become necessary in Nice and its surroundings due to a surprising and unforeseen change.

The situation had radically changed when the Germans crossed into the free zone on November 8, 1942. In this new configuration, the

Italians controlled a portion of the zone, extending from the Rhône to the Alps. Our journey to Nice, then under Italian occupation, was fraught with uncertainty and danger.

ChapTER 9

Clandestinity in Nice

The area we had to cross was essentially under Italian military control. The Italians' attitude towards Jews was notably different from that of the Germans and the French police, offering a form of protection. This policy had created a refuge, attracting many Jews threatened by the occupation to safety zones, including Nice and its surroundings, as well as other regions like Grenoble, Megève, and Saint-Gervais. This haven was almost surreal amidst the chaos of war but had become a beacon of hope for many.

Our journey to Nice, under Italian occupation, was fraught with uncertainty and danger. I traveled by train with the two young people, passing through a zone controlled by the Germans, which was a perilous stretch between Marseille and Aubagne. Fortunately, the control went without major incident. Upon arriving in Nice, I was struck by the sight of groups of Jews gathering in the streets, speaking Yiddish and engaged in lively discussions. The location, a synagogue, was buzzing with intense activity. The owner, unhappy with the commotion, had complained about the synagogue being turned into a sort of station, as it had become a rallying point for Jews arriving in Nice.

Nice itself was captivating, especially in spring, with its beauty and vitality. I even considered the possibility of not spending my later years in Nîmes, drawn by the charm of this new city.

Back in Nîmes, I was faced with a new task. The local Jewish community needed matzot, the traditional unleavened bread for Passover, which were unavailable in Nîmes but could be found in Nice. Having already traveled there, I was asked to go back and bring them.

After the Germans occupied the free zone on November 8, 1942, the situation in Nîmes, particularly for Jewish refugees, became precarious. Many fled, including my parents, who left the city with neighbors and sought refuge in Camarès, a small village in the Aveyron.

I returned to Nice to purchase matzot and successfully brought them back to Nîmes, also preparing a specific package for the Jews in Camarès. These efforts to provide matzot were more than just a gesture of solidarity; they were a vital link to tradition and a form of resistance in a world in turmoil.

In Nice, I sought employment in a shoe factory and found a position with Mr. Mario Simon. After settling my commitments in Nîmes, I returned to Nice and started my job, mounting shoes by hand and hammering nails.

In Nice, I naturally sought contacts within the Jewish community, which was not too difficult. Most activities took place at "Dubouchage." The city was a relative paradise during the occupation. If a Jew was arrested by the French police, a call to an Italian military officer would result in their immediate release. Even the militia couldn't cause harm. There were many activities organized by Jewish youth movements in Nice, with harmonious and close collaboration between the Éclaireurs Israélites de France and the Zionist youth movement. I joined the EIF but also participated in the Zionist youth movement meetings. We sang a lot and discussed news from Palestine.

I began my activity with Keren Kayemeth LeIsrael (KKL) in Nice, around May-June 1943. The Jewish Scouts of France and the Zionist youth movements had launched a project for planting trees in Palestine. We were asked to collect money for this cause. I managed to raise enough funds to plant five trees, which I was very proud of. This is to show you how extremely complex things were. At that time, Joseph Fischer, one of the leading figures of KKL, lived in Nice. He played a very important role in the transfer of funds from the Joint Distribution Committee (JDC). It was then that I met him, very briefly, as I was then a rather insignificant young man. We would meet again later. All these activities, of course, had a huge impact on those who, like me, were evolving in this environment at the time. I also participated in a summer camp of the EEIF near the Col d'Allos.

Indeed, I returned to Nice when events took a decisive turn. The announcement of the armistice between Badoglio's Italy and the Allies led to great anarchy and instability. The Italians in place had ceased to protect the Jews, leaving a part of insecurity weighing on all of us. It was during this troubled period that I realized how vulnerable we were. This perception of our vulnerability and the imminent increase in danger contributed to intensifying my efforts to join my parents in Aix-les-Bains, where Jewish activity was still strong at that time. Nevertheless, my return to Nice and consequently the growing threat marked an important stage in my journey and in my understanding of the war and the fate of the Jews in Europe.

While I was living in Nice at the time, I was not fully aware of the extent of the activities carried out on Rue Dubouchage. I knew there was significant Jewish activity, but the details, the names of the people involved, and the actual extent of their efforts were largely unknown to me. It was only later, after the war, that I learned of their true importance and their precise roles, which made me realize the true scope of their work during the Occupation.

In Nice, there was already clandestine activity aimed at helping young Jews. This was organized jointly by the Jewish Scouts of France (EIF) and the MJS (Zionist Youth Movement). The leaders of these two groups, Jacques and Léa Weintraub for the MJS, Jacques Marburger and Jeannette Ewselmann for the EIF, had already helped many foreign Jewish youths threatened to take shelter.

Now it's September, at the time of the armistice, when German troops invaded the Italian zone. The Italians, not leaving quickly enough, were violently expelled by the Germans. But even before the German troops arrived, a Gestapo commando, in black front-wheel drive cars, arrived in Nice and began a relentless hunt for Jews. The context became more and more dangerous, transforming our lives and our daily activities.

Indeed, in the Italian zone, at Megève and Saint-Gervais, forced residences were established for foreign Jews. When the armistice was signed and the Italians left the place, the Italian authorities, with whom these Jews were in contact, advised them to follow them to Nice, from where they would be taken to Italy to find refuge. All these families then rushed into buses to get to Nice, where they occupied furnished residences and hotels.

It is easy to imagine how easy it was for the Germans to arrest these Jews under these conditions. In addition to the many refugees already present in Nice, the city was overwhelmed with new arrivals. The Germans proceeded in two stages to arrest these people. At first, they attacked the hotels, where the arrest of Jews without proper papers was easy. Even those with false documents were easily recognizable by their accent and physical appearance. To facilitate the task, the Germans were accompanied by Frenchmen capable of distinguishing foreign accents.

The black front-wheel drive cars of the Germans roamed the streets of Nice and when they spotted a person with a suspect physique, especially a man, they stopped. They then took the man into a doorway, made him lower his trousers, and checked if he was Jewish or not. The papers could be falsified, but their method was infallible.

The Germans took control of seemingly safe places - cinemas where people thought they could hide because they were not on the street, restaurants, and neighborhoods where Jews had settled. The most notorious place was what was called the Musicians' Quarter, which included Rue Rossini and its surroundings. These streets were filled with furnished apartments full of Jews. The Germans quickly understood where they had to look for Jews.

Once arrested, the Jews were gathered at the Hotel Excelsior, near the station. From there, they were sent almost daily to Drancy in convoys.

The UGIF office, which served as a center of assistance for needy Jews, was turned into a trap. The Germans forced the director, a certain Guggenheim, to stay on the premises. People who came for help, having no more money for food, were arrested on the spot.

The Chief Rabbi of Nice, Rabbi Pruner, was arrested during a funeral at the cemetery. All the people present were deported at the same time as him. It was a real hunt for Jews, conducted with frightening efficiency. The Germans were guided by no form of ethics or humanity in their actions.

Our efforts at Dubouchage constituted our immediate response to urgent needs, a response that was coming to an end. This mutual aid was fueled by numerous small actions and financially supported by organizations such as the Federation of Jewish Societies of France, which provided subsidies and, when possible, false papers to those in need. These gestures, although informal, represented a vital activity in the turmoil of the time.

However, this precious assistance ceased, leaving a void for those accustomed to relying on this support. In the streets, people searched in vain for support, direction, someone to turn to. It was a period of profound disorientation where the usual structures had vanished.

Despite the challenges, a form of organization emerged, although I cannot describe exactly how it happened. What I clearly remember is the meeting held on September 13 at the Hôtel Chardonnens in Nice, where the elders of the youth movements met. We had to decide on our next plan of action.

There were about twenty of us, united by the necessity to respond to this crisis. There, at this meeting, responsibilities were allocated, each being entrusted with a specific task.

The Weintraubs were part of the group. For the organization of the EI, Claude Guttmann and Griffon were present, the latter having been assigned to lead the 6th in Nice. It was they who took responsibility for the activities being set up.

Léa Weintraub shared a striking memory from the early days of the German occupation: while walking down the street, a Jewish man approached her. He confided in her his intention to help the Jews. This man was Maurice Loebenberg. By a completely fortuitous coincidence, Maurice, who later took the name Maurice Cachoud according to his false identity, was involved from the beginning in the actions undertaken.

The events took a tragic turn with the arrest of Claude Guttmann. He was captured in a monastery on Rue François Grosso, following a denunciation suspected to be the work of a double agent named Anne-Marie Kielissi. She, known for providing false papers, had connections with a police commissioner in Marseille and delivered identity cards from the 8th district of the city.

Claude Guttmann's relatives later learned that he was supposed to go to this convent, precisely to organize a refuge for people in danger. The Gestapo was waiting at the door of the monastery, ready to arrest him upon his arrival, which casts heavy suspicion on Anne-Marie Kielissi, possibly the only one informed of this visit. Guttmann was taken and deported by the Gestapo.

Indeed, I had met Guttmann once or twice. I distinctly remember September 28, a tense day for all of us, especially for the two Jacques – Jacques Weinraub and Jacques Marburger. That day, they were apprehended by the Gestapo and taken for interrogation. Fortunately, their false papers were convincing, their forged identities held up under the pressure of questions. To our great surprise, they were not subjected to a thorough physical check, which could have revealed their deception.

Finally released, an uncommon and unexpected situation, they found themselves free. But it was as Jacques Weinraub was leaving that he suddenly remembered he had left his briefcase in the interrogator's office. Risking peril again, he went back to retrieve it. The unexpected opening of this briefcase could have revealed compromising contents, but fate decided otherwise.

As for Jacques Marburger, known under the totem of Colibri, his name may not be familiar to all, but he quickly fled. He found refuge for the night at my place, knowing he could count on my address in case of necessity. After a night of rest, offering little relief in such circumstances, I lent him my bicycle the following morning so he could get to the station without attracting attention. He thus left Nice and, against all odds, managed to escape his dire fate.

The plans hatched at the Chardonnens meeting in Nice were compromised. The group was almost decapitated, suffering severe blows that could have ended our efforts. How we managed to meet again a few days later at a generous lady's house, I do not know. But the main thing is that we had a rallying point, proof that resilience and the solidarity network were still active.

We met in the house of this lady, whose name escapes me and whose only detail is that she was not Jewish. Someone among us must necessarily have had her address.

In this impromptu meeting, Henri Poriles was there, Maurice Cachoud as well, along with Maurice Beugelmans and Pierre Mouchnik, who had already started his work on false papers – a crucial activity for our movement. There were also women whose names I can no longer remember today.

Despite adversity, Maurice took the initiative. He assumed the role of leader and began to restore order, distributing tasks and responsibilities. Everyone received their mission, their part to play in this clandestine struggle, in this organization that had to adapt and resist in times of crisis.

Maurice entrusted me with a clear responsibility: that of financial management. "You, you will do the accounts, you will hold the cash box," he told me, insisting on the importance of accuracy. "I want exact accounts because one day we will have to account for the money we have used." The task was not the simplest, but it was crucial. In these times of uncertainty, transparency and trust were essential to maintain the integrity of our network and ensure its operation.

We were able to rely on the generosity of those who had been helped by our efforts. Many, after receiving a forged identity card that offered them a semblance of security, were ready to express their gratitude. Their donations were a testament to their recognition and contributed to the common effort. Maurice, for his part, had managed to raise funds from his circle of acquaintances, people he trusted. Each time it was a sum vital for the continuity of our operations, for the purchase of equipment, covering unexpected expenses, and supporting those who were under our protection. Managing the funds meant much more than simply keeping track of numbers; it was about preserving the essence of our commitment and preparing to defend our actions when the time came to account for them.

A few days after Rosh Hashanah, the atmosphere was still heavy from the tragic events we had recently experienced. The community was marked by these difficult circumstances. However, when Yom Kippur came, we were able to organize a tefilah, a prayer, at Maurice Cachoud's uncle, Maxime Polak's home. It was a moment of contemplation but also an opportunity to gather outside the usual context of our clandestine activities.

The prayer meeting took place in an atmosphere marked by seriousness and solidarity, owing as much to religious tradition as to the necessity to maintain our cohesion and morale in these dark times. At the end of the Yom Kippur fast, we were warmly received by Madame Polak who had prepared a meal to break the fast. I remember that moment clearly: the relief of breaking the fast, the warmth of a community sharing the same trials. The journey to Maxime Polak's house was not easy for me; I had gone there on a bicycle taxi, a form of public transportation at the time that included a passenger seat at the back of the bike.

After the meal, accompanied by a dozen, perhaps fifteen other people, we all decided to walk back. Our walk through the streets of Nice took place at night, taking care to respect the curfew. It was during these times, as we silently shared the calm of the sleepy city, that the community found its strength, the sense of belonging, and the determination that pushed us to continue, despite everything that could happen. The day after Yom Kippur, we met again at the Polaks'. All day long, a group of us devoted time to discussion and planning, aware that with each of us assigned a role, it was essential to ensure effective coordination.

We are now in October 1943. The city of Nice is under German occupation, and round-ups are a daily threat. I was still living in my furnished room, run by two very respectable ladies. They never questioned me about my origins or religion, but I sensed that they guessed I was Jewish. Our exchanges rarely went beyond trivialities; nevertheless, their discreet silence amounted to a form of protective complicity. I continued my routine: work in the morning with my employer, and in the evening, I devoted myself to managing the accounts for our organization.

To adapt to the situation and to maintain a structure in daily contacts, we had to develop an organized system. Some young girls and young men, who could be considered as clandestine social workers, brought me lists. These contained the names of people in need, information about their situation, thus determining the distribution of funds. I had to rely on this information to allocate resources. Of course, this remained a complex exercise and necessarily imperfect. The logistics of our meetings had to be meticulous to prevent any detection by the enemy.

Every day, we would meet at a different location, a routine constantly changing for security reasons. This arrangement worked well, demonstrating the ingenuity and flexibility of our network to overcome the challenges of the occupation. We had established an efficient system for transmitting information and requests for false papers, thanks to our contacts with the dedicated team producing these essential documents. The fake papers lab, overseen by Pierre Mouchnik, was a central part of our operation, and everything was done to keep its location and activities secret.

Serge Karvaser was also involved, although he could not risk showing himself in public due to his very recognizable appearance. Requests for false papers were handled with remarkable efficiency: we transmitted the orders, and, depending on the complexity of the work and technical contingencies, the documents were ready in one to three days. However, practical problems sometimes arose, like the shortage of forms for identity cards, temporarily interrupting our activities. Fortunately, the team often found solutions to procure the necessary materials, an area where Maurice was particularly active.

Beyond identity documents, supply was another critical challenge for our proteges. Ration cards, essential for buying basic necessities like bread, butter, milk, and even clothing, had to be regularly updated with new tickets at the town hall. This process required presenting a valid identity card, an impossible and dangerous act for those who had to remain hidden, those who often did not speak or spoke little French and could not afford to be identified. Faced with this obstacle, solutions had to be found to help those in hiding access essential goods without compromising their safety. Solidarity, ingenuity, and discretion were more crucial than ever to ensure the survival of those we were assisting.

Maurice demonstrated remarkable skill in establishing contacts with employees from the supply service. Thanks to these connections, we were able to get ration cards with blank stamps and tickets that we distributed to our charges. Those who dared to show up to renew their ration cards could use their fake documents to do it themselves; for others, who risked too much by coming out of their hiding places, we procured the essential tickets for them. I still recall Suzy, an employee who was both charming and sympathetic, brought to our cause by Maurice. She confessed to us her readiness to do everything in her power to assist us, moved by the prospect of a child suffering or getting arrested simply because they were hungry.

Her words were colored with sincere benevolence. Another invaluable ally, whose name escapes me, as well as the assistant director of the supply service, a certain Mr. Morenon, also extended facilities to us. Morenon confided in us that he was grateful to act meaningfully on a human level, which was of great importance to him. These testimonies of solidarity have been crucial to our action. On a side note, I came to know a young Alsatian named Pauline Dreyfus, index head of the Cub Scouts, who put me in touch with Georges Bloch, a jeweler originally from Strasbourg who had fled to Monte-Carlo. She was convinced that Mr. Bloch could help us raise the necessary funds for our cause.

The major challenge remained reaching Monte-Carlo, a heavily controlled region, but help and generosity coming from various sources were rays of light in the darkness of the Occupation. To get to Monte-Carlo the first time, I chose to take the train from a station somewhat distant from downtown Nice, called Saint-Roch station, in an attempt to remain unnoticed. The journey went without incident, and once I arrived, I met Georges Bloch. His reception was warm, and he expressed immediate trust in our cause and me. He also mentioned a friend, Elie Cohen, originally from Montpellier, whom, by a surprising coincidence, I also knew. The reunion was enjoyable, and both men agreed to solicit their network of acquaintances, also refugees in Monte-Carlo, to contribute financially to support our activities. Convincing well-off people to assist us was not an easy task, caution and skepticism were often the order of the day, particularly in the face of relatively unknown young people. Conscious of this and the need to enhance our credibility, I decided to ask Maurice to accompany me on a subsequent visit to Monte-Carlo.

His charisma and persuasive power indeed made a strong impression on Georges Bloch and Elie Cohen. Thanks to him, our potential supporters became more generous and invested more substantially in our cause. The financial contribution from Monte-Carlo became a precious resource; it allowed us to provide for the needs of our charges and wait on other funds. Speaking of amounts, the exact value is difficult to estimate today, due to the evolution of purchasing power and currency. At the time, a sum of 10,000 to 20,000 francs represented substantial assistance. Although it may not be considered a large fortune, it was enough to meet our immediate needs and continue our support and survival efforts during this challenging period. Maurice, among the young people in our group, distinguished himself through his already abundant life experience. He had run a duplicate agency for the Gestetner company, which gave him a lot of confidence. Trained in sales techniques, he had a natural eloquence, an ease in convincing others, combined with a warm and friendly approach.

This know-how, his ability to communicate, and inspire trust, were significant assets in our clandestine activities. Rooted in a strong family tradition, he grew up in a traditionalist community in Montevideo in Paris, in a most welcoming Jewish atmosphere. His awareness of his Jewish identity was acute, which is certainly what propelled him to act spontaneously for the Jews when he understood the situation was becoming critical. He cared for his father, who was also hiding in Nice after the death of his mother. He had to live in the shadows to care for him while taking on a leadership role in our collective. His ability to always get to the heart of the matter was remarkable. He made it clear to us that our aim should be direct and practical action, without getting lost in political discussions or unnecessary debates: action had to be taken, and quickly.

Superfluous details were not our concern. His presence was spiritually comforting; he knew how to find the right word for each person and give courage to everyone. His aura was not that of someone who goes unnoticed, on the contrary, he stood out on the street, which makes it even more astonishing that he was never stopped or arrested. That was fortunate, or perhaps proof that Providence was watching over him, as it did me. His divine protection, for those who believe in it, seems to have played a very real role in our lives. I circled around Nice on a bicycle, and why I chose one street over another during round-ups remains a mystery. Luck was on my side; I was never stopped for an identity check. In the climate of insecurity, I obtained a false identity that we created with the means at our disposal.

According to the information on this identity card, I was born on January 15, 1915, in the Chapelle Blanche in Savoie, and my name was Rosna Maurice - a name that had no reality for me. When asked why I was never arrested, I would jokingly reply that my "Aryan" appearance probably worked to my advantage, suggesting my looks did not align with the stereotypes sought by the authorities.

The documentary base to create this fictitious identity was a demobilization sheet for a French prisoner of war from the camps in Germany. This lent additional credibility to the document. As far as the robustness of this false identity in case of control, it would all have depended on the intensity and rigor of the control. If the services were executed, specialized in counter-espionage or members of the Gestapo, and they had undertaken thorough verifications, they could discover that though the name existed in the commune where I was supposed to be born, it would not withstand a meticulously conducted investigation. However, I must say, in all honesty, that this card was never put to the test during a control. It was a mix of luck, presence of mind, and perhaps as some like to think, providential intervention that enabled me to evade such perilous situations.

German controls at the time did not usually extend to in-depth investigations, except in the case of serious doubts about someone's suspicious activities, such as espionage or participation in resistance activities. The important thing was to be able to pass through checkpoints without arousing suspicion. As for Maurice, he was indeed born in Paris. His family had various origins: his father was German, and his mother had Dutch roots. Maurice's maternal side, the Polak family, was Dutch Jewish but had resided in Paris well before the war. And if my memory serves me right, his mother was born in the French capital. His father, on the other hand, was in France from the period that followed World War I, since Maurice was born during this war, which means his father was already on French soil even before the war.

Concerning their parents' professions, Mr. Polak, Maurice's uncle, was a banker. Maurice's father likely worked with him. They did not own the bank but held significant responsibilities within a small private Jewish bank in Paris. The Polaks were indeed relatively well-off. A few days after the Yom Kippur tefila that we spent at their home, tragedy struck: Mr. Polak was arrested on the street and then deported. Fortunately, it seems he managed not to disclose his address, perhaps thanks to papers that did not directly link him to his home, as his wife and children were left undisturbed at home afterwards.

During this same period, besides the Cachoud network, there were also other clandestine networks active in Nice. Among them was Kelman Fajgenbaum, later known as Claude Kelman, who later played a significant role within the FSJU and was one of the founders of the CRFF. Showing great bravery, he had set up a support network for people in need, but a lack of caution led to the arrest of one of his assistants, and Kelman had to hide in Monte-Carlo.

There was likewise the considerable presence of Mr. Rogovski, a non-Jewish Russian, who had been a minister under Kerensky's socialist government before the Bolshevik Revolution. Fleeing Russia for Paris, he and his secretary, Olga Bax-Mars, greatly aided both Jewish and non-Jewish Russian refugees. Another network led by André Bass also made efforts to provide false documents and financial assistance. André Bass had likewise to leave Nice following his detection by the authorities. Despite the presence of these different networks, our group found itself at one point to be the only operational one in Nice, a situation that represented a double-edged sword of responsibility and risk in a dangerous context.

Joseph Fischer, upon the Germans' arrival, left Nice for Lyon. Indeed, it was challenging to establish or reestablish contacts to acquire the necessary funds for our work. About a control experience I had, contrary to what I might have said earlier, there was one. It was between Christmas and New Year when I was going to Aix-les-Bains to see my parents. Having to change trains at Grenoble, and having an hour and a half to wait, I impulsively and perhaps recklessly detoured through the city.

I was strolling through Place Grenette in Grenoble around 4 p.m., when suddenly I heard a small explosion followed by flares, the signal for the German troops to close all exits and proceed with a mass control. Caught in the moment, I headed straight for a German non-commissioned officer at the barricade, explaining to him that I needed to catch my train and, while opening my bag, showing him my identity card and postcard. To my great surprise, he simply indicated that I should pass. I had spoken in French, not caring whether or not he understood me properly, simply insisting on the fact that I had a train to catch. It was an incredible stroke of luck because many Jews were caught in such roundups and sent to the STO, Soft Labour Force. It was a moment of great tension but also of great luck, a rare event that marked my experience at that time.

Circling back a bit, during the winter of 1942-1943, when I was still in Nîmes, laws on the Compulsory Work Service (STO) had been promulgated by the German occupier. This mobilization forced young people to sign up to work in Germany. I remember asking several people for advice on what to do: some said it was necessary to sign up to be in compliance, while others advised against it. Ultimately, I did not heed the call, thus remaining off STO's radar, fully aware that any control could lead me, at the very least, to a work camp in Germany, even before my Jewish identity was revealed.

After the incident in Grenoble and my visit to my parents, I returned to Nice. Then, in January, Maurice made contact with Maurice Brenner, who represented the Joint in occupied France, based in Le Puy, a prefecture in the Haute-Loire department. We took the train to meet Maurice Brenner in Le Puy, not Puy de Dôme, but the city of Le Puy in Haute-Loire. Maurice Brenner's reception was very warm, and he allocated us a significant amount, I remember it well, up to 100,000 francs. Although these funds did not last forever, they nonetheless represented a significant contribution that allowed us to somewhat improve the living conditions of those we were assisting.

Indeed, we had lengthy discussions with Maurice Brenner. The situation was extremely precarious at the time. The winter of 1942-1943 was marked by uncertainty, and the Battle of Stalingrad was not yet resolved, and the victory of the Soviet forces had not yet materialized. The overall situation was rather dark, with no palpable flickerings of hope. Confidence in the future relied more on blind faith than on tangible arguments. Nevertheless, we tried to encourage each other to keep hope.

During this same period, in Nice, the Franc group was formed, parallel to our own activities. This group, over which I had no direct responsibility, was led by Henri Porriles. The main mission of the Franc group was to identify and neutralize denouncers who collaborated with the Gestapo, often motivated by money. In Nice, a group of White Russians had tragically made a name for themselves by denouncing hidden Jews for their own profit.

The task of the Franc group was then to physically eliminate them and intimidate others to deter them from continuing their malicious activities. These actions were not simple and met with initial difficulties, but over time, they managed to put an end to the actions of some of these denouncers, and to instill enough fear for others to cease their betrayals.

ChapTER 10

The resistance groups

The Franc group was a designation for a resistance cell. It consisted, among others, of Henri Porriles and his brother Isidore Porriles, but also of Annette Zisman. There were other members whose names I don't remember all. These details can sometimes escape memory over time. Regarding the meeting with Maurice Brenner in Haute-Loire, we did not know him personally beforehand. Maurice had a recommendation to facilitate contact. Brenner didn't just take us on our word, he conducted a real interrogation to get specific details about our activities and needs. We provided him with lists of beneficiaries with their signatures to prove the legitimacy of our requests.

It was thanks to the serious recommendation that Maurice brought that we were finally able to gain Brenner's trust. Without it, it would have been difficult, if not impossible, to obtain his financial support. The recommendation served to convince Brenner of the authenticity and seriousness of our cause, which was essential for establishing a financing channel for our resistance activities. Brenner apparently had the funds in person, which is not surprising given the circumstances and banking restrictions of the time. Normal financial and banking transactions were obviously compromised by the war and occupation. Cheques and bank transfers were out of the question, everything was done in cash and under the table.

It's possible that the money was physically handed to Maurice and he then passed it on to me, but I can't remember for sure. The details of this transaction are fuzzy to me. However, whether it was 100,000 francs or some other amount, transporting such a sum of money was a significant risk. Brenner asked for reports of our work, but understand that we could not afford to carry detailed documents about our activities. This would have been extremely dangerous. We certainly provided summary information, detailed enough to reassure him about the use of funds without compromising our safety. At that time, one had to be very careful about what information was shared and how it was shared. Despite this, we managed to convince him of the legitimacy and importance of our cause.

We indeed kept in touch with Maurice Brenner after our meeting, although I never saw him in person again. Brenner's financial support represented a significant "oxygen balloon" for us at that time, although we didn't receive any further funds from the Joint afterwards. We continued to raise money in Monte-Carlo, and it is largely thanks to this funding that we were able to maintain our operations. As for the 100,000 francs, we did not distribute this sum lightly. We made out monthly budgets in order to last over time. This sum, however, did not suffice to cover our needs until the end of the war, but without it, and without the additional support from Monte-Carlo and occasional donations received in Nice, we would have had difficulties to continue.

Those who received forged documents from us sometimes contributed financially, even though we never asked for anything in return. We simply pointed out that if someone could afford it, their donations could help provide documents to people without resources. It is important to remember that those who made the forged documents and the social workers needed to survive. Although we couldn't talk about a salary, we allocated subsistence funds to cover basic needs, such as food. There was a uniform scale for everyone, calculated to allow the purchase of sufficient food for a month. Beyond that, no one could count on our help for clothing or rent, for example. The means were limited, and we had to manage these resources very carefully to ensure everyone's survival in our network.

The hazards of memory are indeed relentless, and they can sometimes play tricks on us, especially after so many years and significant events. The need to correct and supplement what we have forgotten is understandable, particularly when it comes to paying tribute to the people dear to our personal and family history. The time of the war, starting in 1939, was heavy with consequences and mourning for my family. The death of my maternal grandmother in October was an expected loss due to her old age and illness.

The tragedy was prolonged in December with the death of my cousin Suzanne, who was only 20 years old and who died of puerperal fever following her childbirth, a devastating event that occurred under the care of a doctor. Then, in January 1940, my aunt Mathilde, my father's sister, succumbed to stomach cancer. I remember the exhausting ordeal that was her funeral, forcing us to walk the 6 kilometers between Lingolsheim and the Wolfisheim cemetery under difficult weather conditions, with snow reaching 50 to 60 centimeters. It was a time both emotionally and physically painful.

As for Montpellier, it seems that I locate my memories there not in 1942 but rather in 1941, although the dates start to blur slightly with time passing. These moments of personal history can be hard to trace accurately, but it's important to gather them together as much as possible to form a faithful narrative of this lived experience. It is precious to remember these fundamental learning moments, even in such troubled times. The teaching of Rabbi Schilly and Mr. Kolodny was a pillar in learning the basics of Hebrew. The courses they taught were about more than just language lessons, as they embodied a connection with our heritage, our culture, and our identity.

It is vital not to forget the figure of Rabbi Hamburger, who initiated so many people into the Gemara before being deported, zekher tzadik livracha, may his memory be a blessing. Their teaching and passion for the Torah and the Talmud were illuminating and motivating despite external circumstances.

Mr. Kolodny, in particular, was able to awaken in us an interest in the texts of Shoftim (Judges) and Shmuel (Samuel), offering us a deeper understanding of Hebrew grammar. His patience allowed us to grasp different binyanim, or verbal constructions, such as Kal, Piel,

Hifil, and Hithpael, as well as rules of syntax and pronunciation such as Vav hahipuch and stress accent.

This period of study has a particular resonance for me, as despite the war, it represents a memory of personal effort and self-discipline. During my stay in Romans, during the first half of 1942, while I was at cobblery school, I devoted myself to studying every night. Armed with a Humash and a Tanach, in my narrow, unheated room, only a 25-watt bulb illuminated my writings, a concession of the landlady. These memories of solitary study, under such modest conditions, are a reminder of resilience and commitment to preserving knowledge and tradition despite challenges.

In Nîmes, Rabbi Swal introduced me to a precious rite: the Kriyat Hathorah. I managed to read it, that of the Parshat Shemini, in the local synagogue in a certain month of March 1943. The attendance was sparse, but one must understand the context of the times, marked by the oppressive presence of German patrols. Every daily act was imbued with palpable tension, and the act of faith represented by this community reading was almost reckless.

It is also important to remember the particular situation of the Italian zone of Nîmes, a subject already mentioned. The leniency of the Italian authorities did not stem from spontaneous generosity. Angelo Donati, an Italian Jewish banker established in Nîmes, played a decisive role in this. His persistent efforts and influential connections with the Italian military were fundamental in drafting and maintaining a policy of protection for Jews, despite pressures from the Vichy regime, the threat of militias, and the constant surveillance by the police forces of the National Revolution. Many owed their survival to his action and commitment.

Donati, a figure I never personally knew, but whose reputation preceded his never-seen silhouette. His ambitious plan was to facilitate the transfer of Jews from the Italian zone to Italy. Yes, I believe I have discussed this topic before. The courage or, to be precise, the lack of bravery of the Italian soldiers was tested with the advance of the German troops. Their hasty flight abruptly ended all evacuation attempts orchestrated by Donati, thus making his project fail.

It was in September 1943, a period marked by dark turns, notably by the arrival of the Gestapo, synonymous with increased terror. At that moment, Saint-Martin-de-Vésubie became a residence-forced place for foreign Jews not yet caught in the whirlwind of deportation. Fate, arbitrarily, separated these refugees into different paths: one group was able to cross the border and take refuge in Italy while another fell into the trap set in Northern Italy to be deported subsequently.

As for those who escaped the net, they owed their salvation to the tenacity and assistance of Italian partisans. They survived, clinging to every moment of freedom, blending into the shadows of secrecy. Each of their breaths was a tenacious resistance against oppression, a struggle for existence even in the darkest hours of our history.

It was at the same time, in September 1943, that the tragic story of Jeannette Ewselmann unfolded. She, who was a scout in Nice, along with her own was captured in the unforgiving vice of the just-arrived Gestapo. Fortunately, or perhaps due to a mixture of prudence and fear, she carried a false identity. This stratagem allowed her to escape from the Hôtel Excelsior, turned temporary prison for arrested Jews. She was able to taste freedom again, a liberty tinged with pain, as her family did not have such luck and was swept away by the black whirlwind of deportation.

I also elaborated on the story of Mr. Mario Simon's shoe workshop in Nice where I had found occupation upon my arrival in the city in 1943. Despite the shadow of my increasing clandestine activities from September onwards, I maintained my post with Mr. Mario Simon regularly. However, as the end of the year approached, in December 1943, I was forced to abandon this laborious cover. I had to devote all my time and efforts to the resistance, the struggle becoming too overwhelming to allow for a double life.

In February 1943, I remember our comrade Ernest Appenzeller, who had been incarcerated since December, managed to avoid a tragic end in Drancy by assertively claiming to be not Jewish but Christian. By means unknown to me, a baptism certificate was passed to him, resulting in his release in February 1944. One can easily imagine the wave of relief and intense joy that flooded him upon regaining his freedom, a joy shared by us all, happy witnesses to his return to Nice.

As for my adventures in Nice, I remember, albeit somewhat vaguely, the restaurant of l'Abbaye Saint-Paul in the old town. I'm not sure if I've mentioned it before, but this place was emblematic in our lives. I believe it was Maurice Cachoud who had managed to get on the good side of the owner. L'Abbaye Saint-Paul became a refuge, an extension of our daily universe. We indulged there in Nice-style pasta dishes, a priceless luxury at the time as they were served without requiring ration tickets—a pure and simple pleasure in the context of wartime deprivation.

But the restaurant also played a riskier role, that of a small arms cache. It was not without danger or discomfort, but I must admit that the staff at l'Abbaye Saint-Paul showed remarkable understanding and support. These were acts of discreet resistance but of crucial importance, which I wish to highlight and recall with gratitude.

I did not go to l'Abbaye Saint-Paul every day. These visits were limited; after all, we still had to pay for our meals, even if it was without ration tickets. We met there one to three times a week. And yes, the managers were quite aware of our activities, even if the subject remained taboo, discussed only in undertones. They were strongly pro-Gaullist, which engendered an affinity and mutual understanding of our intentions and resistant actions.

The financial situation of the people we were helping was becoming ever more desperate. However, new hope loomed when the city hall of Nice organized an evacuation program to rural areas where food was more accessible. We immediately took advantage of this boon, orchestrating the departure of numerous families. Moreover, the evacuation documents issued by the city hall added further credibility to their false identities, thus consolidating their security. By February, there were still some 430 people under our responsibility. I would now like to speak about Pastor Evrard. After the war, in 1945, Evrard was called to testify about his clandestine activities. His testimony was solicited by several entities, including the center of Nice's city hall, the city of Paris, Spain, and the documentation center of Nice. His involvement and role during those dark years were therefore recognized and documented, a tribute to his courage and contribution to the clandestine struggle.

In the statement of Pastor Evrard, poignant details are reported on his commitment, how he met and supported Raymond Heymann and Maurice Cachoud, the leader of Jewish resistance in Nice. He describes how he and his sons actively took part in the assistance of persecuted Jews. They contributed to the safekeeping and supply of the persecuted, with a courage the incessant danger of which cannot be ignored. From identity cards to the hospitality offered, their actions were fires burning in the darkness of oppression.

He also spoke of organizing the celebration of the feast of Purim in his temple, where the reading of the Megillah constituted a moment of strong symbolism and deep spiritual elevation. This event took place against all prudence, on a Wednesday in late afternoon, where the faithful arrived by bicycle as if to mark the everyday but with a unique resonance of defiance. Evrard remained among his own, while his sons oversaw the safety of the gathering.

Admitting their consciousness of the reality of war and the critical situation in which they were, they were nevertheless capable, for one evening, to transcend fear and immerse the participants in an atmosphere where thought elevated beyond oppression. The parallels with the story of the Megillah could not be more poignant, placing each participant in front of the mirror of a contemporary tragedy, where each read word echoed with their own struggle for survival and liberty.

Every gesture, every gathering, every action was imbued with danger during this period. Pastor Evrard had grasped this well; investing his temple in the struggle and making gatherings like the celebration of the feast of Purim, was going all in. It was a bit like attempting a risky maneuver at bridge, an impasse: one had to accurately evaluate the risks to take, those that could be justified and those to avoid at all costs.

It seems that moving around in the city or going to Rue Vernier was not in itself a significantly greater risk than any urban movement at that time. However, if the Gestapo had carried out a raid during one of these gatherings, the consequences would have been devastating, without a shadow of a doubt.

As for the number of people present, we were nine men, accompanied by the young girls. A small assembly, intimately gathered, in search of spirituality and communion despite the weight of the terror hovering over the occupied city. Every meeting, every prayer then carried the weight of resistance, the breath of a subversion against a never-ending night that seemed to envelop the world.

The direction present that day for the celebration of Purim gathered the individuals we had been able to mobilize. What is significant here is the rarity of the gatherings and the risk taken by each of these people, knowing the dangers they were facing.

The testimony of Pastor Evrard provides an insight into other events, like the tragic story of Madame Vera Kogan, who attempted to end her life by poisoning. This story was unknown to your group and your involvement; it is an anecdote exclusively reported by the pastor. It seems that she was hospitalized and then left as long as possible in Pasteur hospital to protect her. But eventually, she was brought back to the Hotel Excelsior, where the Gestapo had set up its headquarters.

The meeting with Gérard, one of the Gestapo's leaders at the Hotel Excelsior, highlights the psychological dyad within this terrifying organization. On one hand, Evrard describes Schulz, a calm and polite man, yet known for his sadism, based at the Hôtel Hermitage. On the other, there is Kraus at the Hotel Excelsior, a personality described as mad and extremely brutal, known for his terrifying outbursts of anger and violent interrogation methods. As for Eckerle, he appears as more moderate, forming a counterpoint to the first two. Gérard, though crude and impulsive, seemed to have some influence over Eckerle, and although primitive and rude, he was capable of "good movements," perhaps clemency in certain circumstances.

What these anecdotes illustrate is the complexity and danger of the situation for the resistants and the Jews in Nice under occupation. Every action, every meeting, every gesture was charged with tensions, and the personalities encountered could represent the difference between life and death.

In his encounter with Gérard, an influential member of the Gestapo, Pastor Evrard used a strategy of talking about a past where he had dedicated himself to the reconciliation of nations, highlighting his supposed aid to the Germans before the war. This narrative seems to have been imbued with humanity and persuasion, with the aim of defusing tensions and manipulating the situation in favor of Madame Kogan. Although skeptical about her chances of release, the pastor used his emotional intelligence to evoke a responsiveness in Gérard, who was presumably German. To his great surprise, and thanks to the intervention he had initiated, Madame Kogan was released and directed to him to express her gratitude.

As for Maurice Cachoud, his fame beyond Nice was well established. It was not he who manufactured the fake papers but played a pivotal role in facilitating contacts between the various local resistance movements and the National Liberation Movement (MLN). His capacity to provide papers from the local laboratory via the city's economic channels had extended his reputation to Paris. This assigned him to assume national responsibility for the MLN's counterfeiting laboratory, a position that summoned him to Paris.

The case of Maurice Cachoud highlights the complexity and flexibility of Resistance activities. While the counterfeiting laboratory in Nice was operational, Maurice Cachoud was responsible for organizing a new workshop in Paris. Even if he did not start his project from scratch, since resources and structures were already available in Paris, his contribution was to make this workshop more efficient and operational, capitalizing on what was available.

What distinguished Maurice Cachoud was his organizational capacity, his audacity and, in Yiddish, his "chutzpah" – this extraordinary boldness and vitality, which left a strong impression. He was known for opening doors that others would have deemed closed, often flirting with almost incredible recklessness. This indeed played regrettable tricks on him later, even though at the same time he was always extremely concerned about the safety of those who worked with him.

Regarding communication with Maurice post-February, contact was not lost, but communications naturally became more complicated and less frequent. Without a telephone and in a time when discretion was vital, connections were often made through movements between Nice and Paris for various reasons. These trips were an opportunity to exchange information and maintain a link, although it did not have the regularity of an organized correspondence.

After Maurice Cachoud joined Paris to take over the counterfeiting laboratory, I remained in charge of the social assistance sector, while Henri Porriles was more focused on the self-defense group. Concerning the militant and direct actions of this group, I will tell you a description given by Henri Porriles about an operation carried out by the franc-group.

Henri Porriles's narration describes an ambush organized against Georges Karakayev. This man, of Russian origin, divided his time between artistic painting and the more serious activity of denouncing Jews to the enemy. A strategy of spying and seduction by a young girl in the group allowed them to corner him and set a meeting. On the agreed day, the girl appeared, but she did not come alone – the armed members of the franc-group were ready to act. They proceeded to action on bicycles, and quickly, the informer was neutralized.

When I think about how many targets the franc-group could thus eliminate, I can't provide an exact number and I prefer not to speculate. This data must be recorded in the testimonies of the participants in the various operations, in which I did not take part. It was especially Henri's brother, Isidor Porriles, known as Zizi, who was active in these missions. He was a key executors in this device, although he was not the only one.

Among his-comrades-in-arms, there were Annette Zisman and Marc Levy, the latter joined Israel in 1948 where he died during the War of Independence, as well as Lucien Rubel. These were the main team members I remember, but I may be forgetting some.

As for Ernest Appenzeller, mentioned earlier, he also took part in these operations. Truly, he was also part of this combat, this clandestine struggle carried out with courage and determination. Zizi, his real name Isidor Porriles, and Ernest Appenzeller indeed formed an active pair within the Resistance, although I wouldn't say they were inseparable. They worked closely and effectively as a team, each having a role to play within the operations to carry out.

From April onwards, the arrests and denunciations orchestrated by the White Russians - these anti-communist Russian emigrants - decreased, although the danger of such betrayals persisted until the landing in Provence. As for the specificity of the franc-group, what characterized them were probably the personal traits of its members which inclined them towards such high-risk activities. Some were naturally inclined towards bold, operational actions, while others were more turned towards assistance and support. There were those who had the audacity needed to face peril, and then there were those who, without weapons or means of defense, risked just as much by acting in the shadows, often abandoned to their own devices and very vulnerable.

The youth who engaged in clandestine assistance, not only in Nice but throughout France, were often inexperienced and confronted with immense danger, sometimes without the ability to defend themselves. These young people exposed themselves to considerable risks and, indeed, often had "the jitters" in the face of these risks. Courage is not only measured by the ability to face danger while armed; their devotion was just as noble and their actions just as heroic.

Finally, I would mention the arrest in early March of my uncle, Louis Hallel, in Montélimar, and the miraculous rescue of his family who, warned by neighbors, were able to hide and join my parents in Aix-les-Bains. This demonstrates the solidarity and mutual aid that played a crucial role in survival within a hostile and dangerous environment. Each action, big or small, bears witness to the resilience and courage of those who lived through those dark times.

As Passover approached, the question of matzot became acute, in a context where each element of tradition took on even greater importance. It was thanks to the ingenuity of our comrade Jacques Neufeld that we were able to overcome this obstacle. He managed to obtain flour and found a biscuit factory that we could make kosher. This allowed us to make the necessary matzot, which were distributed by our assistants before the Passover celebration.

During a trip to Le Puy, made in January, I had the opportunity to meet Jean Poliatschek, the son of a rabbi from Altkirch in the Haut-Rhin. I invited myself to his place for the start of Passover and the Seder. Armed with my matzot that I had carried in my backpack, I went to Le Puy. There, Passover began with the Seder in the back room of a restaurant, where we recited the Haggadah, paced in the background by the noise of the boots of Mongolian soldiers from the German army stationed in the town.

The next day, despite the threatening environment, a tefila took place in a discreet location and we enjoyed nature in the afternoon. This experience was particularly exhilarating, demonstrating the determination of Jewish youth to assert, even in adversity, even provocatively, their Jewish identity and their belonging to their people. A spiritual resistance that, in the darkest moments, takes on its full meaning and becomes an act of rebellion and preservation of Jewish cultural and religious heritage.

My parents were indeed in Aix-les-Bains during this period. As for my choice to celebrate Passover in Le Puy rather than with them, it was dictated by safety considerations. At that time, traveling to Le Puy was a lower risk than joining Aix. This decision, in response to your relevant question, was guided by caution in these uncertain times.

After the Passover celebrations, I headed for Vichy, where I had planned to meet my sister Simone. She was set to travel from Aix to Vichy, and our intention was to visit together the cousins who were hiding in Châtelmontagne, near the town. However, on arriving at the Vichy train station, I received a disturbing welcome, as my cousin, who we were supposed to visit, informed me that the Gestapo had searched her home and arrested her sister. Faced with this situation, it was no longer possible for us to go to them. Simone therefore decided to return directly to Aix-les-Bains, while I hid for a few days at the home of cousins living in another town to avoid being caught in the Gestapo's net. It was a time when the slightest decision could have fatal consequences, and vigilance was our constant companion.

The farm in Châtelmontagne where my cousins and my Uncle Herschel were hiding represented an exceptional haven of supply, providing them with a comfortable quality of life under these difficult circumstances. They enjoyed a relative freedom, being able to navigate within the boundaries of the farm and the immediate surroundings of the hamlet.

Although they had a certain freedom of movement within this perimeter, they were discreet about their identity. Living conditions did not involve constant seclusion within a limited space but a limitation on the public display of their presence and Jewish identity. Indeed, my cousins and my uncle were not confined to a single enclosed space; they were not cloistered in a room or an attic and could afford to go out.

ChapTER 11

The Jewish survival

However, the safety of their situation depended largely on the complicity and discretion of their neighbors. Although the latter suspected that these new "farmers" were not from the region, their pro-Gaulle attitude made them reliable and they offered their tacit support.

The reality of Jews hidden in France during World War II presented a wide range of situations, which sharply contrasted with what one might imagine by referring to cases like that of Anne Frank in the Netherlands. In France, if some were heavily confined, others adopted borrowed identities to blend into their environment. On the whole, people's ability to hide and maintain a form of anonymity varied greatly, ranging from semi-autonomy to more severe restrictions on their freedom of movement. Individual character played a decisive role in how each person managed their security during this period of persecution.

Some, by nature more audacious, sometimes took too many risks, which led them, tragically, to deportation. Others, more cautious, also paid a heavy price; audacity could not be singled out as the sole cause of capture by the Germans. During the large raid in Nice, those who were informed avoided walking in certain streets, notably in the Musicians' Quarter around Rossini street, which was a preferred target for the Germans. The main axes of the center, Victory Avenue (now Jean Médecin Avenue), and the surrounding streets, with their shops and places of life, were particularly risky and absolutely to be avoided. With the months and the decrease in raids, a certain form of relaxation in vigilance occurred, following the principle of communicating vessels.

For my part, for months, I had forbidden myself to frequent Victory Avenue, but by the end of spring 1944, this reservation became less strict, for better or worse.

As part of my coordination role with the social assistants, my many trips were concentrated in neighborhoods considered less dangerous. I traveled by bike, thus avoiding overly exposed areas. As for the arrest of my uncle Louis in Montélimar, which occurred in early March – an event I have already mentioned – my aunt and cousin Hubert had to flee to Aix-les-Bains to find refuge with my parents. This episode illustrates the precariousness and urgency of the situation for many Jewish families at the time.

My uncle, deported following his arrest, unfortunately experienced a fate that many others shared. Facing this imminent threat, my parents decided to cross the border into Switzerland. My young cousin Hubert was first sent by a children's convoy in early April, a relatively common procedure at the time to try to get children to safety. Then, my parents and Aunt Blanche followed them at the end of the month. They were interned in Switzerland, as their internment card dated May 26, 1944, indicates.

My sister Simone, for her part, supported herself under a borrowed identity in Chambéry, where she worked for the "Aide aux Mères" organization. This charitable association offered its support to families who had welcomed a newborn, providing assistance for baby care and household chores related to this arrival.

As for crossing to Switzerland, the organization relied on discretion and perfect knowledge of the terrain by local smugglers. They had to be experts in the paths and informed about the schedules of German patrols to increase the chances of successful crossings. In return for their services, these guides were paid, although the passage was often postponed due to the increased presence of German troops at the border. Eventually, they led people to a certain point before leaving them to continue alone.

Concerning the group of children Hubert was integrated into, the exact details of the organization of this convoy escape me, but there were many initiatives at this time, often ad hoc, run by organizations like the Children's Aid Society (OSE) or more informally, with groups of children transiting through different routes to get to Switzerland or elsewhere in safety.

Yes, there was indeed a certain level of coordination among the various organizations that dedicated themselves to the rescue and transfer of Jews, especially children. Despite this, the precarious situation and the individual circumstances of each person often required private or personal initiatives rather than purely organized actions. Indeed, organizations like the Israelite Scouts (EI) and the Zionist Youth Movement (MJS), as well as the Children's Relief Fund (OSE), conducted structured and highly organized operations to transfer children, but the great variability of contexts and needs implied a great diversity in the methods used.

To cross into Switzerland, one had to find a smuggler. My sister made contact with one to help my parents cross the border. The smuggler chose the opportune moment based on information he had about German patrol schedules, guiding people to the border before pointing them in the right direction to continue alone. As for the children organized in groups to cross the border, although I do not have all the details, it is certain that several groups were formed and passed through different networks and organizations, some of which could be ad hoc, with no fixed affiliation to a rescue structure.

Upon my return to Nice in April 1944, I witnessed a heartbreaking scene at the Abbey of Saint-Paul. Monique Picard, an acquaintance from Montpellier, came in a state of despair to announce her brother's arrest during a raid on a children's home near Grasse. Despite our attempts to send him a baptismal certificate, which would probably have allowed him to be released, confusion about his identity failed to stop him from being deported, as he was registered under his mother's birth name, Cerf, and not under the name Picard on the certificate.

As for my trips to Monte-Carlo, the raids there also created a palpable tension. My contacts, Georges Bloch and Elie Cohen, had to hide themselves too, having attempted a passage to Switzerland, but were arrested. They seem to have been able to pay for their release, although the exact circumstances of this release remain unclear. They changed address in Monte-Carlo to continue escaping detection.

As for access to the beaches, they were forbidden during the war, particularly after the German occupation that had installed fortifications in anticipation of a possible Allied landing. The Promenade des Anglais and access streets were blocked by concrete obstacles. Before the Germans' arrival, the Promenade was a lively place for the people of Nice and the Jews.

Despite all of this, I maintained a personal commitment to Jewish life, and every Sabbath afternoon, I would go study the week's Paracha with Prosper Weil, a teenager whose family from Bouxwiller had taken refuge in Nice. This happened in spite of the proximity of the Gestapo, evidence of resilience in the face of oppression. The Weill family, fleeing Alsace, found refuge in Nice, an internal exile laden with uncertainty and the weight of days. At that time, listening to Free France Radio from London was an act of resistance in itself, given the ban on owning a radio. While I didn't have one personally, I knew enough people where the waves of freedom were secretly captured. The broadcast information reached us, keeping us informed, hoping for the landing during this spring of '44.

News from Italy was bitter; the Allies fought fiercely, progressing at an exasperatingly slow pace amidst a human cost that kept escalating. Mussolini, for his part, never failed to display his usual arrogance. The fate of our deported compatriots was enough to torment us day and night; we feared the unspeakable, never being able to anticipate the true horror of what they were enduring, a reality that surpassed human understanding. It was only after liberation that the truth was revealed to us in all its brutality, a horror surpassing our darkest imaginations.

The shockwave of these revelations had to find counterbalance in solidarity, as the morale of every member of our group suffered. Separated from our families, it was a constant struggle to keep our heads above water, to keep hoping. When news of the landing came on June 6, 1944, it was a monumental relief that swept over all of us, a breath of hope for liberation that shook our hearts. However, this hope did not change our pressing problems: the food shortage was worsening, and arrests continued. At this critical time, we had set up a hotel room as a secret office thanks to the complicity of the pro-Gaullist owners of the Assalit Hotel, located near the station in Nice. That's where Jacqueline Cotliard, acting as secretary, received and redistributed the fake papers produced by the laboratory, essential to our fight for survival.

Despite the pressure, the Assalit Hotel had become a microcosm of resistance, a place almost ordinary on the surface, but the stage for illegal but necessary actions. Caution was necessary; at the slightest suspicious sign, everything was hidden under a mattress. Jacqueline often worked there alone, and we only came to transmit or receive crucial information, and always during the discreet hours of the morning and afternoon.

During this period in Nice, we were looking after about 430 people, a number that had remained relatively stable since the last count. The faces weren't necessarily the same, it's true. Some had been swept away by the terror of deportations, and we had seen new cases arrive. Individuals, hitherto silent from pride or fear, revealed themselves to us, driven by despair. Their reserves were dwindling over time, and the shortage left them no choice but to seek help.

In the past, before reaching this number of 430, we had succeeded in redistributing some refugees to areas where supplies were easier.

After that, despite slight variations, our number fluctuated around 430, and the stakes remained significant.

However, our financial situation was becoming increasingly worrisome. We always kept an emergency reserve, a "safety buffer", but it was decreasing alarmingly. As a result, I made the decision to go to Paris to seek help from Maurice. I found him at the Montpensier Hotel, but the news was not good regarding financial support.

However, I did get a chance to observe the ingenuity and boldness of his work. On the Esplanade des Invalides, at clandestine meetings nicknamed "Cachoud meetings", Maurice orchestrated an intense distribution of fake papers, animating each exchange with passion and urgency. Despite this, our financial means remained diminished. Yet, cruel fate caught us up on July 18. A pernicious betrayal saw Maurice and his companions fall into a trap orchestrated by the double agent Charles Porel. Promising weapons parachuted from England, he led them straight to the Gestapo. Maurice, Ernest Appenzeller, Rabbi René Kapel, and others were captured; despite torture, Maurice revealed nothing.

After this tragic incident, our means of communication were disrupted. We had no direct contact with Maurice's family; his address was unknown to us. It was only later that we learned of his grim fate. A meeting was held on Tisha B'Av, July 30, when we learned the terrible news. It was in Madame Nardi's apartment, at the Roussey-Gouran castle, a place we had always considered safe.

Desperate but resolved to persevere, I chose to try my luck in Monte-Carlo, following an address provided by Georges Bloch. The journeys were difficult, hampered by German military devices, barricades, and mine threats. The destruction of the Saint-Roch station, for its part, had severely reduced rail links to Monte-Carlo, making the task even more complicated.

To maximize my chances, I opted for a scout disguise, hat on head and short trousers. Thus attired, I set off on the road. The journey was complex, interspersed with stretches made on foot and by bus. Eventually, I arrived at the Gessulas' who seemed quite surprised to see a character of my kind turn up. Nevertheless, their welcome was most warm. They were able to give me a small sum of money and committed to try to collect more from their contacts.

On the morning of August 15, I was awoken by the deafening noise of gunfire. Smoke was rising in the distance, a sign of the explosions marking the Allied landing in Provence, especially in the Var. It would take almost two weeks before Nice was liberated. During that time, about fifteen Jews had been arrested and were in the hands of the Gestapo. Transport to Drancy was no longer feasible, the railways being severed. We dreaded the Germans resorting to executions or acts of torture in a final burst of barbarism. Fortunately, all these detainees were released. Our fears proved groundless. Panicked at the thought of being surrounded, the Germans fled in a hurry, without having time to organize more violence.

This period was marked by some confusion; we did not really know what to expect. Was it really the end of the conflict? We knew at least that a decisive turn was near. The intentions of the Allies were, however, not clear to us, their immediate goal seeming to be to move north, leaving Nice a bit on the margin of their march.

It was finally the American soldiers who arrived first, not the forces of the French Resistance. However, the presence of the Germans quickly diminished, partly thanks to the Maquis' action. To what extent did the latter influence the German retreat? Difficult to evaluate, but we were aware of their presence and even had links with several groups to whom we provided falsified documents. These same groups supplied us with weapons for the French fighting forces.

On the 27th of August, we received instructions from our local resistance leader. We were affiliated with the FTP, Francs-Tireurs, and Communist-leaning Partisans, under René Cantat's lead. Thanks to their network, we were mobilized to neutralize the blockhouse on the avenue of the station in Nice. We had received the order to move towards the objective with the utmost caution and to avoid being exposed.

This was no small feat, but we managed to position ourselves at a distance where we could engage the enemy. For the occasion, we had been given weapons - rifles, nothing very elaborate, but it was all we had. As soon as we fired our first shots, the German response was immediate: intense gunfire. Fortunately, we had no casualties on our side. After a few moments, one of our watchmen, posted higher up in a nearby building, informed us that the Germans were abandoning their position, firing to cover their retreat.

About half an hour later, we advanced and, after some additional exchanges of fire, we noted that the Germans had left the blockhouse and retreated. We did not know if they suffered any losses, but the most important thing for us was that all of ours were safe. On the morning of the 28th of August, the news spread: no more Germans in the city. The usual barracks and checkpoints were deserted. The American troops were meanwhile in Saint-Laurent-du-Var, very close to Nice.

I took my bike to the Arenas, west of the city, and found American soldiers, sitting on the sidewalks, refreshing themselves and eating their rations. They looked exhausted, their equipment weighing heavily on their shoulders. When they got up to advance, they walked slowly. So, it was not a triumphant victory parade, but rather the laborious progress of weary soldiers, with no fanfare or ceremony. As to the origin of the American soldiers we met, it is true that I could not answer precisely.

Their background could come from North Africa and include the Italian campaign, but that would require specific military knowledge. As for the directive we had received, it was to rally to Cimiez, to look for the prefect appointed in the underground, a certain Moyon. On the way, I found an abandoned Peugeot that I temporarily requisitioned to follow the procession with a few comrades to the prefecture.

The city was brimming with joy with the inhabitants massed on the sidewalks, showing their joy for this landmark event. Moyon was thus the new prefect of Nice, a socialist designated by the resistance organizations as temporary prefect. The initiative coming next from one of our comrades was to immediately invest the Jewish Affairs police station.

It was completely deserted; we were met by a frightened caretaker who let us take over the premises. This allowed us to transfer our activities from the underground to open visibility. Concerning the archives at the police station, it was not us who took charge of their recovery, but rather specialized Resistance groups. What I could find on the commissioner's desk, which I subsequently occupied as director of the office, were various official stamps, but at that time, the idea of preserving these documents as evidence for possible testimony seemed distant to me, and in the urgency of the situation, it was not my priority.

We had at our disposal a series of offices, and very quickly, Jews emerging from their hiding places came to see us, hoping we could solve their many problems. This was even before we could set up an organized system, and it was necessary to provide them with food. Our boxes were empty, but we miraculously received funds from an unexpected source. I cannot specify where this surprising input came from, but a donation of 750,000 francs from the regional Resistance committee reached us, a sum that proved extremely valuable to cover the most urgent needs of those who presented themselves to us.

The funds we had received were used as emergency relief for the families whose lists we had maintained during the underground period. New cases were revealed on this occasion, and the initial criteria for distributing aid were not clearly established. We had to make quick decisions to provide first aid, in the absence of formal experience in social work. Our approach relied heavily on common sense and the determination of those who improvised as social workers on the field.

As we adjusted to this new reality and our transition to an openly social role, the assistance network also emerged from the shadows. Moussa Abadi, in collaboration with the OSE (Children's Aid Society), had organized a rescue network for Jewish children who had been hidden in Catholic institutions in the region. Benefiting from the support of the bishopric, Miss Lagache meticulously kept the records of those under her protection.

Accompanying Moussa Abadi to the Bishopric one day, I was able to see the esteem and warmth with which he was received there. Abadi managed several hundred children – the exact number escapes my memory, but it fluctuated between 100 and 200, knowing that some had been sent to Switzerland or elsewhere. Moreover, a White Russian, a former member of Kerensky's government, Rogovski, and his faithful secretary Olga Mas, had also emerged from hiding. During the Occupation, they had helped Jews and perhaps also non-Jews from the Russian community.

CHAPETR 12

The martyred Jewish childhood

After the Liberation, the hidden children began to be returned to their families, under the management of Abadi. He also had to settle boarding fees in the host institutions, though I am not aware of the source of his funds. There are certainly orphans who remained, but I cannot provide details on this.

In the Jewish community, with the Liberation, life began to start returning to normal. People were able to start reclaiming their property and finding work again, signaling a slow return to a less urgent existence and less marked by the torments of war.

The crossing from the years of occupation to the post-war period was marked by extremely varied personal situations. Some people were quickly able to resume their professional activities, while others suffered from the fact that their businesses had been entrusted to provisional administrators, and sometimes stripped in the process.

There was no uniform rule for recovering goods and activities. The most entrepreneurial people began to rebuild their businesses where possible, while others encountered serious difficulties. All this unfolded gradually; changes did not happen immediately after Liberation.

The first days of regained freedom were tinged with some confusion and euphoria; it wasn't always clear where to focus our efforts. However, one crucial point remained: providing people with food. The funds we had enabled us to overcome this critical period.

We were young and inexperienced, but Maurice's principles remained firmly ingrained: no unnecessary politics, no vain speech, but concrete actions in response to clear imperatives. For us, it was essential to gain legal status for our activities. Thus, we created an official structure before the authorities, the Israelite Committee for Social Action, which would later serve as a model for COJASOR, the Jewish Committee for Social Action and Reconstruction.

Our formal registration of the association at the Prefecture plunged us into the maelstrom of the political struggles of the time. Prefect Moyon, a socialist, had indeed been replaced by a communist. Virgile Barrel, on the other hand, had taken the mayor's office of Nice by force, and played a key role in the local Communist Party.

Despite a strong presence of FTP and active communists in Nice -who were able to assert themselves by their active presence on the ground- there was also the UJRE, Union of Jews for Resistance and Mutual Aid, which claimed representativeness of the Jewish community. I had to defend our cause in a memorable confrontation at the Prefecture against the communist lawyer, Maître Jacques Lippmann. Although his eloquence was formidable, our mission and vision prevailed over time, allowing us to continue our work in service of the community.

In the period that followed the liberation and the end of clandestinity, the organization I managed did not seek judgement nor to justify itself. We did not insist on our formal registration in the registry of associations either; we simply continued our activities as if nothing had changed. That's why I had remarked that the caravan goes on.

What became clear was that the UJRE seemed mainly interested in the financial resources that we had received. They got wind of our allocation from the regional committee of resistance and since they were short on funds, they were attracted to it.

As for idea that the UJRE could infiltrate our organization, it was unlikely, as most of the young people involved were Zionist and not aligned with the communist perspectives. In fact, we had the support of Maître Edmond Montel, the senior lawyer of Nice, who became the honorary president of our association. His support helped us to continue our mission.

I maintained contact with Monte-Carlo to ensure the continuity of funding while waiting to establish relationships with the Joint or other organizations that were reorganizing at the national level. Our days were not just devoted to negotiations; we were primarily absorbed by concrete social work, responding to numerous requests. We started establishing folders, acquiring the necessary material, creating files, and documentation.

Talking about it, I would like to illustrate with the lists of names that we had during the clandestinity, which I was compiling with fortnightly allowances. You can see the number of people per family and the signatures or fingerprints attesting to the receipt of funds. On one of the lists, you will see the mention "taken" instead of a signature, this indicates a person who had been arrested. The amounts varied, ranging from 300 to 400 francs of that time on average, depending on the number of people per allowance.

In September 1944, I had the first news from my family. My parents were interned in Switzerland and my sister Simone, whom I had not heard from for months, had stayed in Chambéry until the Liberation, then returned to Aix long before them. She took care of a children's home that Rabbi Soal had set up for the children hidden in the region. Unfortunately, many of these children could never be returned to their deported parents.

At the end of September, I also received a letter from Henri Porriles, dated September 4, informing me that he had managed to escape with Ernest after being arrested on July 18. His mother had stayed in Nice, where she had gone into hiding. After that, I made contact with the Parisian organizations gathered within COJASOR to prepare grant applications, as our clandestine resources had been exhausted. People were less available than before because they were now focusing on rebuilding their own lives after the Resistance.

Run by Fink and Topiol, COJASOR became a key player in Paris. Regarding Fink, I'm not sure if he had returned to Nice, but I do know that he had been hidden and then established himself in Paris after the Liberation. I also needed to plan for the salaries of my assistants who obviously could not continue without remuneration and finance office expenses like electricity and heating. Thus, I had to think about how to financially support the infrastructure necessary for our social work in this transition period.

Yom Kippur services went as planned at Boulevard Dubouchage, which gradually regained its usual vibrancy. Among the notable personalities, there was Mr. Dubinsky, the respected president of Dubouchage, and Rabbi Rubinstein, who later became a rabbi in Paris in the Pavée quarter. Before leaving the region, he had taken responsibility for the Minyan Dubouchage.

A painter named Mr. Berzon, recognizable by his traditional style of mustache, as well as the cantor, Mr. Katz, were also well-known characters in the community. During this time, there was also a certain hustle and bustle because of the American presence, with a flourishing black market in alcohol, cigarettes, and canned goods, as one could imagine.

Mr. Katz, his wife and his daughter Yeta, who later joined our team, were arrested just before the landing in Provence. They were among the 15 people who were freed after Gestapo agents had fled following the landing. This was the last Jewish arrest in Nice.

As for the food supply, it remained very limited despite the appearance of white bread. The American soldiers were a significant source of supplies for us. In Nice and its surroundings, which were scarcely agricultural and relatively arid, it was difficult to get supplies, except for a few fruits and olives. Even products like cheese mainly came from the Hautes-Alpes, which were quite distant. The transport networks and fuel supplies had not yet returned to normal.

The building at 15, avenue de la Victoire, had transformed into a buzzing place of activity, where we continued to work to meet the emergency and needs of our community in this era of reconstruction. I faced many incidents with the people we were assisting. We quickly had to start making a selection, based on the information we could gather. We discovered that some of those who approached us for help actually had hidden funds. The number of raucous incidents and confrontations began to increase. I sometimes had to intervene with individuals who started shouting in our premises, threatening to wreck everything if we did not give them money, refuting all the accusations against them.

In some cases, we had to make arbitrary decisions. Otherwise, our body of cash would have quickly run out. This kind of phenomenon was not new, but during clandestinity, we did not have the same control capacities. We had to largely trust the intuition and judgment of our social workers to discern who really needed help and who was exaggerating or did not really need it.

Meanwhile, various social works reemerged. The Consistory reorganized, with notable figures like Mr. Théodore Kahn, Mrs Bader, and Mr Berland. It was at this time that a loan fund was created, thanks to the initiative of Mr. Kowarski, that granted honor loans, allowing many people to restart their professional lives.

The first joint activity with COJASOR in Paris, still called that at the time, was launched under the moral auspices of what had been the CRIF, notably a loan fund to help people in need get back on their feet after the war. This was a difficult period of rebuilding, where we had to balance immediate aid with the necessity of promoting autonomy and the economic restart of the beneficiaries.

The CRIF, Representative Council of Jewish Institutions of France, is a representative organization that was reorganized after the war. Indeed, on the initiative of Mr. Berland, honor loans were made, which greatly contributed to support the reconstruction and mutual aid in the Jewish community.

On my return to Paris, the CRIF got involved in various projects, notably giving its patronage to a Jewish childhood martyr week. In this effort, support vouchers were sent to a Jewish childhood martyr to be sold. I was given vouchers of a value of 5 and 10 francs, which seemed rather derisory to me; I did not believe that we could gather a significant sum with such small amounts.

So, I took the initiative to have vouchers printed in Nice up to 10,000 francs, which we started selling. We had some success in this enterprise, but what was particularly striking is that we obtained the agreement of the education inspectorate for these vouchers to be sold in all the schools of the Alpes-Maritimes department, of course, at smaller amounts.

This campaign was a way not only to collect funds but also to raise awareness among young people about recent history and the sufferings endured by Jewish children during the war. This was a period where solidarity and Holocaust education took a central place in the efforts of rebuilding the Jewish community and French society as a whole.

During this period, our efforts to support the Jewish childhood martyrs were strengthened by the support of Mr. Virgile Barrel, the mayor of Nice, who had agreed to come to launch our campaign. This event was even relayed by a local journalist, increasing the visibility of our action. This activity took a lot of energy, but it also allowed us to collect a substantial sum. Naturally, the collected funds had to be sent to the national committee; we did not have direct disposal of them. The most crucial aspect, however, was raising awareness among the non-Jewish population of the drama of the Jewish childhood martyrs.

I also obtained special authorization from the chancellery of Monaco to sell these vouchers in the principality. This was an important step to extend our action beyond Nice and reach an even larger audience. For the distribution of these vouchers, I appealed to everyone - all those who were ready to help us. In schools, the sale of vouchers was organized with the cooperation of the academic inspectorate. This was a time of solidarity and commitment, demonstrating the shared will to rebuild and remember, in the wake of the darkest period of our history.

Just after the end of clandestinity, while I was still young, I began contemplating the future and discussing the various options before me. Naturally engaged in action and propelled by strong ideals, the idea of going to Palestine emerged as a major aspiration. This period was marked by intense reflection and debate within our group, and to nourish this intellectual and militant fervor, we published a small typed monthly journal for three or four months that we called "Tekhelet-Lavan". This journal was the vehicle for many positions, sometimes critical of the responsibilities of the Jewish community on the national level. We accused them of not having sufficiently helped the hidden Jews during the war.

I remember drafting an open letter addressed to the Chief Rabbi of France at that time, Isaïe Schwartz, in which I asked him rather directly to make way for more active individuals. We felt the need for a renewal within the community's instances, for new and entrepreneurial energies capable of breaking with established routine and bringing new perspectives.

As for the collection of funds through the childhood martyr's vouchers in schools, with the agreement of the academic inspectorate, unfortunately, I don't have exact figures to give, not having found traces of this amount. But this awareness-raising effort will remain for me an important moment of reconstruction and commitment to collective memory and justice for the youngest victims of the Shoah.

Against the tragic backdrop of news coming from the deportation camps, which reached us little by little, we realized the true extent of the disaster. The worst fears that we had imagined proved well below the terrible truth. The deportees only started to return after the armistice, during the summer of 1945, but information had leaked out in the meantime.

At the same time, youth movements, such as the EI (Éclaireurs Israélites) and others, were bustling with activity. We quickly noticed a dire lack of educational material, particularly a songbook. Songs are vital in youth movements; they are the heart and soul of collective spirit and camaraderie. Many of us knew a lot of songs, but no one knew them perfectly by heart, and there was no reference document.

I took the initiative to print a songbook, with active help from Prosper Weil, whom I have previously mentioned. Naturally, the booklet was printed in Latin characters. We began transcribing songs, with French translations of the lyrics just below. Very quickly, we were able to print these songbooks in 500 copies. This was an important symbolic project which played a key role in preserving our cultural heritage and transmitting the values of our community to younger generations, in the collective effort of rebuilding after the war.

I found the invoice for the songbooks that had been printed on the presses of the newspaper "Le Patriote niçois", and its edition was called "De l'Aurore". The order had been placed by the Zionist youth movement, for which we had printed 500 songbooks. Reviewing my calculations from that time, I had determined that we wanted to keep 50 songbooks for youth movements, for the leaders, and we planned to sell the remaining 450. I had taken care of defining the cost price by dividing by 450, the invoice being dated 22 December 1944.

We also organized a Hanukkah party that year, which was extremely successful. We were fortunate to have amongst us a group of siblings, the Pomeranzs, who were tireless and gifted at organizing public celebrations. They made the Hanukkah party absolutely remarkable, making this occasion vibrant and joyful for many people who had lived in hiding during the war. These initiatives were essential to reviving our community and provided necessary moments of comfort and sharing after the dark period we had just gone through.

The Hanukkah party was the first opportunity to socially reconnect with Jewish tradition after the war. It was an assertion of our identity and a comforting time for all of us. Also, I had inquired about a group of refugees located in Cuneo, Italy. This group had managed to leave France with the Italians in time and had been able to maintain themselves, as I had already mentioned in previous discussions. I had planned to visit them, having already obtained all the necessary passes and authorizations, but, unfortunately, the military authorities closed the border, and I could not go to Cuneo.

During the winter, we had to deal with numerous material problems. I want to acknowledge the Roux family, non-Jewish friends of Jeannette Ewselmann, who supported us by being proactive in the cause of liberal France and very favourable to Jews. Their support was invaluable.

I also want to express my gratitude to the Katz family who welcomed me into their home with extreme kindness. The Friday nights I spent at their home, in an atmosphere suffused with singing, remain a strong and warm memory.

Upon Jeannette Ewselmann's return, she joined our group and also contributed to our social activity. With Passover approaching, the matzah was baked by a specialized baker, Mr. Mrowka, a Jew who owned a biscuit and matzah factory even before the German occupation. The only difficulty was the allocation of flour, which we eventually managed to get for him.

These periods of Jewish holidays were occasions to strengthen our sense of belonging and to continue the work of rebuilding the Jewish community after the terrible trials of the war.

Then came Passover 1945. During this period, my parents returned from Switzerland and resumed their furnished accommodation in Aix-les-Bains. It is important to underline the kindness and friendship of their landlords, Mr and Mrs Blanc, who had taken great care of the items left by my parents, and did so with discreetness essential during the Occupation.

As for a return of my family to Strasbourg, it was envisaged, but hostilities of the Second World War were not yet over at that time. There had indeed been the Ardennes counteroffensive, a crossing of the Rhine by the Germans, and nothing was yet certain about the outcome of the conflict.

So we decided to organize a collective Seder for Passover, which required rigorous supervision, notably that of Rabbi Songalowski. This was a considerable undertaking: an entire kitchen in a large downtown restaurant had to be koshered, and our whole team pulled together for the success of this event.

In regard to the number of Jews remaining in Nice at that time, it is difficult for me to give a figure, even approximately. During the Occupation, estimates were made of around 30,000 Jews in the region, but in my opinion, this figure is somewhat exaggerated. I would rather say that we were around 20,000. And I even think that many have left the region since then.

We believed that several thousand Jews had been arrested in Nice and the Alpes-Maritimes, but in reality, according to documents established later, there were fewer than a thousand who were arrested and who went through the Excelsior camp in Nice. It's possible that people were deported directly without going through the Excelsior, and in that case, they aren't included in this statistic, but the figure was much less substantial than the scale of the round-ups might suggest. Of course, even one arrestee is too many, and our thoughts were with each one of those who suffered.

The Passover Seder was a great success, although the assistants were impatient, eager to "leave Egypt" and eat the meatballs. This is a very human reaction; despite everything, most of the participants showed their satisfaction. Jeannette Ewselman played a crucial role in the organization of this Seder, and we were able to celebrate this success with a walk in the spring dawn of Nice, which marked the beginning of our engagement. I would like to revisit an incident that did not occur in Nice but deserves to be mentioned. Before the Liberation, I went to Marseille, during the period of the American bombings. To tell the truth, I don't exactly remember the reason for my visit, but I had been recommended to contact two Alsatian families there. Out of the four people, it turned out that there was only one Jew.

André Weingarten lived with the Merius couple; Mrs. Merius and her sister, Hélène, who was André's fiancée. Mr. Merius and he had found work with the Todt organization, which allowed them to get through the period of hiding. However, they were denounced by neighbours who accused them of helping the Germans. Following this, they all got arrested. Mr. Merius and Hélène were later released, but Mrs. Merius died after her release, while André Weingarten remained in detention, where he was tortured and died in prison.

I eventually learned that behind this tragedy stood Anne-Marie Kielitschi, a double agent who, while she was working in Nice in September 1943, was a friend of a policeman in Marseille. It was she who caused the downfall of André Weingarten, who was perfectly innocent. The work he was doing for the Todt organization was purely manual, as a laborer and truck driver.

CHAPTER 13

A return to Strasbourg

Strasbourg was liberated on November 23, 1944. Of course, my parents and I were eager to return to see what remained of our apartment on rue du Général Gouraud and our shops. In early May, an opportunity arose: a refugee from Colmar, Mr. Kahn, had a car, a small Rosengart. We made an arrangement: he didn't know how to drive, so I would drive him to Colmar and then go to Strasbourg to check the state of our property. Afterwards, I would come back to pick him up for the return journey, as he also had a clothing shop in Colmar that he wanted to check on.

By the way, we went to pick up my father in Aix-les-Bains in order for all of us to go to Strasbourg together. I will not dwell on the technical incidents, like tires and wheels, which considerably lengthened our trip through the Alpine road. After having to spend the night in Digne, we finally arrived in Aix-les-Bains, collected my father and continued our journey to Colmar then Strasbourg.

We were aware that American bombardments had heavily damaged Strasbourg, with numerous bombs having destroyed close to 3,000 houses, and therefore about 12,000 apartments in September 1944, two months before the city was liberated. Our apartment in rue du Général Gouraud was occupied by American G.I.'s who seemed to have celebrated with numerous bottles of cognac. The bombings had left only the walls of the apartment intact, all the woodwork had been ripped out by the inhabitants in order to heat themselves during the winter amidst a coal shortage.

As for the shop on Grand-Rue, it was occupied by a usurper whose own store had been destroyed by the bombings; but regardless, he had taken over our shop. It was a difficult return to Strasbourg, tinged with sadness, powerlessness, and melancholy.

Tuesday, May 8th, the armistice was declared while we were in Strasbourg, marking the end of hostilities between the Allies, USSR and Germany. If the end of the nightmare promised a period of peace, the joy was tempered by the anxiety of what we would discover about returning deportees, in what state would they be found?

My cousins Max and Paul were prisoners, while the third, René, had managed to be repatriated. On Wednesday evening, May 9th, we found ourselves in a cafe on rue du Jeu des Enfants, where returning refugees met to exchange news. It was a place full of emotions where people, more or less acquainted, would share their stories, seeking comfort with each other after the endured hardships.

Indeed, it was mostly Jews who met in this cafe to exchange news. During this meeting, my cousin Paul, who had been repatriated to Paris the day before and had just arrived in Strasbourg, found me. It was an incredibly moving reunion. I had not seen him since his mother's funeral in the snow, at the beginning of January 1940. He was in good shape; he had been working with farmers in Austria and therefore was physically fit. His brother Max returned a few days later, but I had already started my way back. I drove Mr. Kahn back to Colmar, dropped off my father in Aix-les-Bains where we made a stop, and took my sister Simone to Nice to spend a few days. This would also be an opportunity for her to get to know Jeannette. My parents returned to Strasbourg in July.

This was also the period when my age group was called under the flags. I was hoping that we would be overlooked. I did indeed have a demobilization card, but it was not in my name. What subsequently happened is that our age group, having served only several months of military service – which wasn't really one, as we were part of the youth worksites –, was recalled to serve in units tasked with guarding Axis prisoners of war.

I finally managed to put forward my title as a Resistance lieutenant, which was accepted, at least for a time. In the end, I managed to maintain my rank as a second lieutenant, positioning me in a command function rather than among the rank and file.

Indeed, after being called to Marseille to join the armed forces, I was able to get a letter from the president of social works of the Alpes-Maritimes, orchestrated by my deputy in Nice, Jacques Inouefeld. The letter insisted on the fact that I was playing an absolutely indispensable role in Nice for the smooth running of the Jewish Committee of Social Action, and that my activity fell within the framework of the essential missions of the region's social assistance services. Thus, a transfer to the 445th company guarding Axis prisoners was requested for me— a transfer that was supposed to allow me to perform my vital functions for the community outside of service hours.

When I arrived in Nice, I quickly felt useless and thought that others could take over to guard the Axis prisoners. I simulated an illness, which earned me admission to the Mont-Boron hospital. The doctor didn't seem too inquisitive, and after visits, I would slip away to go to the office. Nevertheless, I had to return for the night due to the evening roll call. Despite everything, I was succeeding in getting the bulk of the work done at the office.

With the return of the deportees began a period and a reality of unspeakable horror. We knew that many deportees would never return. We feared that most would not return, but we were far from imagining the true extent of the horror of the Nazi concentration and extermination camps, the gas chambers, the crematoriums, the tortures, the immeasurable suffering endured before their annihilation. The return of a few surviving deportees completely unsettled us; their stories traumatized us in such a deep way that it is hard to describe.

Facing these survivors, we felt completely powerless in the face of their own trauma. Between us there was a gaping chasm, an abyss dug by the horror and suffering they had endured. And despite the material aid we were able to offer—though insufficient—it was impossible to bridge this gap, this vast distance shaped by experiences that only those who had truly lived them could understand. It was a reality that we had to confront, knowing we would never be able to fully alleviate the pain or understand the extent of the losses suffered by those who returned from the hell of the camps. I am genuinely sorry, but I cannot give an exact number of deportees who arrived in Nice. I can't remember if it was 20, 30 or 15, these details now escape me.

As for their accounts, people found it very difficult to speak. Their experiences were so painful and traumatic that finding the words to describe them was often insurmountable. The authorities set up a structure, the COSOR, specially dedicated to helping the repatriated, among them many resistants. The survival and return rate of deported resistants was indeed higher than that of deported Jews. It is crucial to clarify that these are proportions, not absolute figures. There were also forced workers coming back home after the war. All these returns required intervention by the authorities and the COSOR did remarkable work in this regard.

Nevertheless, the main difficulty was to deal with the lived experience of the repatriated, an experience often incommunicable and unbearable for them to bear. Many were returning without their families, without their children or their parents, and each case represented a terrible and unique tragedy.

I would now like to present some documents. Among them is my card from the French Forces of the Interior, which was, of course, established well after the Liberation. On this card, you can see that it is affiliated with the FTP group of René Cantat Logan Martin and Jean-Marie. It is a vestige of my commitment during these dark years, a commitment that cost us dearly but also inspired us with a tremendous will to resist and liberation.

During the clandestine period, we had established contacts with the FTP (Franc-Tireurs and Partisans), and we continued to collaborate with them during the Resistance. This card is linked to my activity for Tchadacheni, a commitment that I will explain in detail later, but you can already see that there is a text in Russian and the flags of the Allies as well as the Russian flag.

On this card indeed, my role as the head of the social service and the laboratory of the Resistance is listed. This department was in charge of providing identity documents, rationings, in other terms food supply, and intelligence. Even though we were an integral part of the FTP militarily, we also maintains relationships with other resistance groups. Our main contribution was the fabrication and distribution of false documents, while they provided us with the necessary weapons on Liberation day.

Josée was the eldest of our social assistant group. Her exact age was unknown to me, she kept it a secret, but she was probably between 45 and 50 years old. Jacqueline Cotillard, Mika Niagouche and I were all younger. Mika Niagouche, German by origin, was extremely skilled and committed in her work. The photo of our team is only a representative slice; several collaborators were missing.

The time came when I had to hand over the committee's leadership to Jacques-Henri Feil. Our links with Paris were now established, and we could count on the assurance of budgets for assistance and salaries. November was the month for me to return to Strasbourg, to rebuild the family business. My father had confided in me that without my help, he would not have the strength to start over alone, and that if I did not come back, everything he had built would be lost. Thus, the Aliyah will have to wait for about a quarter of a century. Jeannette also headed towards Strasbourg, where she would stay with her uncle Lucien Cronbach and his family. Our wedding was planned for the spring of 1946, as soon as we could find a home, a complex task given the numerous destructions in the city.

It was a time of rebuilding and major changes, not only for me personally, but also for the Jewish community and the entire country, recovering from the ruins of this devastating war. The material devastations could not compare to the human tragedies caused by the Holocaust: mourning the deportees who would never return, the indelible sufferings etched in the hearts of those who survived. We all mourn the comrades who lost their lives in the fight alongside us, pavers of the path, examples of courage and resistance. At that time, our dearest wish was to be worthy of their sacrifice and never to forget their fight. It was a principle we tried to embody in our actions and our daily lives.

When I look back today at that period and the war years, it is difficult for me to draw lessons or formulate a judgment about these terrible years. You ask me to undertake both a psychological and historical study, which is a daunting task. What is sure is that this period deeply marked all of us. For my part, I lived an intense and often demanding life experience, but I cannot say that it was in vain.

These experiences, although laced with pain, have shaped who I am and influenced the course of my life. They are anchors in my memory, constant reminders of the darkest realities of our history, but also evidence of resilience and the human spirit's capacity to seek light even in the densest of darkness.

There's no denying that we would have preferred to avoid the trials of war, but they have left indelible marks on us. Personally, I emerged from this period changed, with a perspective far removed from what I had before the conflict. Between September 1939 and November 1945, I have delivered a largely incomplete account, and I am well aware that I have failed to convey the intensity of these years, marked by daily dramas, mistakes, gropings, moments of despair, and fleeting victories.

Our deepest gratitude must be expressed to our loyal non-Jewish friends, whose help and dedication were vital to our work and our survival.

As for the question of the significance and importance of my activity during the war, it is true that I could do vital things like save lives and provide crucial assistance without which some people would not have survived. Moving into daily routine after a period of such traumatic and critical actions can be difficult for some, but personally, I do not believe I experienced too strong a shock or disillusionment. I feel that I managed to move from one phase to another relatively naturally, although the challenges I faced after the war were of a very different nature than that of the Resistance.

It was imperative to rebuild after the war, and this was done under the best conditions possible, despite the inevitable mistakes anyone can make. I then headed the KRN-KMH in Strasbourg for 25 years, a role I dedicated a significant amount of time and effort to, for the community's benefit.

On May 19, 1946, the French Forces of the Interior awarded me the Resistance Medal. It was a great source of pride for me for 20 years. However, following the stance taken by General de Gaulle in November 1967 after the Six-Day War, I felt it necessary to return this decoration. I expressed to him my inability to keep an honor emanating from someone who had betrayed the trust that a small state like Israel could place in him. I drew the parallel that, just as France had previously betrayed Czechoslovakia, it had just betrayed Israel. The decoration no longer had a place in my home, especially after the general's comments about the "sharp, proud, and dominant people."

I am glad to conclude this conversation and thank you for reading. I sincerely hope that this testimony can be useful, both to my family and to researchers who might be interested in consulting it in the future.

This is a wish that I make from the bottom of my heart.

About the Author

Raymond Heymann (1919-2009) was not only a key figure in the Jewish community of Strasbourg but also a prominent member of the French Resistance during World War II. His courageous efforts earned him the Resistance Medal from Charles de Gaulle. Post-war, he continued to contribute significantly to Jewish life, eventually making Aliyah to Israel. His legacy also includes his recorded testimony for Steven Spielberg's Holocaust archive, preserving vital historical accounts for future generations. This multifaceted life of service and dedication to Jewish culture and history makes him a notable figure in both French and Jewish history.

9 798224 876129